# Men are Dirt

# Men are Dirt

## SPIRITUAL INSIGHT FOR HEALTHY RELATIONSHIPS

*by*

Timothy Houston

Houston Publishing

All scriptures unless otherwise noted are quoted from New International Version (NIV) of the Bible.

# Contents

# Dedication

This book is dedicated to women of all ages and from every walk of life. It represents the best of me, and it comes from the good that is stored in my heart. May it bless you!

# Introduction

THE writing of this book has been a test of endurance that began six years ago, and involved various computerized catastrophes including a corrupt floppy disk, two lost memory sticks, and three hard drive crashes. Despite these major setbacks, I refused to quit. I will never forget the year-long trips to the library where I retyped the first seven chapters, and after the first computer glitch, rewrote the last five from memory. I can now reflect back, with a degree of equinity, on the nights and weekend at Starbucks rewriting and refining the book after the three hard drive crashes. Bolstered as I was with resilience and resolve, I was determined to finish despite any and all obstacles. And my readers should know that I never intended to rush to publication. From the onset, I was determined to take my time in order to share my spiritual insights with as much clarity as possible.

The road to the completion of this book has been a wonderful journey of self-discovery and I am a better man because of it. I can only hope that this will serve as a catalyst to others facing their own challenges. Why the determination? Why a book titled Men are Dirt? These are two key questions are tied together by the same response. Because things that come from the heart take time to reach the surface, I was primarily concerned with maintaining a consistent theme, one which I felt was most clearly encapsulated in the title that I finally chose.

The title captures the spirit and intent of this book. Men were formed by God from the dust of the earth, and as we know, the quality of this earth itself differs greatly. More important still, it nourishes seeds that will become plants or metaphorically speaking, ideas. The best of both man and the earth from which he was formed lies below the surface in that both can nourish. The sooner we can be brought to understand the spiritual and creative connection between earth and man, the better we will be able to understand man himself.

The inter-workings of the mind, body, and spirit of man are so complex that many of the books written about this subject are extraordinarily difficult to follow. This is why I decided to simplify the approach to the subject by using the analogy of the earth representing the heart of man, as well as his soul. The seed is the good that will be planted in it. The stems or vines are the thoughts that come up out of man and extend themselves to others. Because these thoughts are generated by his heart, rich soil will produce a good harvest, but if the soil contains no nutrients, it will be barren.

Although I speak of men, this book is written with women in mind, particularly since women will always be the primary participants in any relationship. This book is intended to empower them by making a clear distinction between the many and various types of men. A separation that will allow them to choose only those relationships that will add enrichment to their lives. For those women who are currently in relationships, my intent is to help them to better understand the men in their lives. The better a woman understands a man, whom they cannot control, the more she is empowered.

This book is also written from my perspective as a man, one who understands other men and the challenges they face. It is based on biblical principles. The Bible speaks for itself, and I intend to provide you with the associated scriptures so that they may speak directly to you as well. I know firsthand what happens to a man when his spirit is positively impacted by God's word. By sharing my personal experience, I offer you an opportunity to benefit from what I have learned as I freely and openly share the wisdom my heart has gained from having listened to the word of God.

## Chapter 1

# All Things Begin and End with You

*I make known the end from the beginning… My purpose will stand,*

*(Isaiah 46:10)*

## TO THY OWN SELF BE TRUE

*I am the captain of my soul (William Ernest Henley)*

I can remember, years ago, as a young man, reading women's magazines trying to get insight on how women thought men should behave, and I was amused. I was pretty convinced that none of the writers were men, but despite this conviction, over time I modeled the image they projected. If it was a "Cosmo man" they wanted, then it would be a "Cosmo man" they would get. I would do whatever was necessary to get women to respond favorably to me. In the process, I hid the real me, certain that the less women knew about how I thought, the better off I would be. In time, I learned how to use the image women had of me to my advantage. This became my game of shadows. I became a chameleon reflecting the expectations of my environment.

Although this game of shadows was a negative approach to relationships, as a young man, it was the only one I knew. To make matters worse, the game became more and more destructive over time. Shakespeare wrote in Hamlet, "To thy own self be true." This was a profound statement that I took to heart with the result that I no longer projected a false image of myself to win the favor of others. By being true to myself, I was able to attract people to the real me.

Over time, as I matured, I learned to be true to myself. This was not easy, but the journey was well worth it. I decided to use my personal experience as well as the experience of others to write a book relating man to his basic and fundamental composition, dirt. This book gives the reader the information needed to make an informed decision about men. It gives the reader spiritual insight from a man's point-of-view. This book contains some of men's best kept secrets and unspoken rules, revealing their true nature. This insight will provide the reader with choices, which is very important because the choices one makes can change our lives. And when it comes to changing your life for the better, all things begin and end with you.

Before you can be true to others, you must first be true to yourself. You will always be the constant in your relationship. You are numeral uno and the numerator in your relationship equations. When men bring spiritual, emotional, and financial value equal to yours, the relationship becomes one or whole. On the other hand, when their baggage is greater than your resources, the relationship becomes a fraction of what it should be.

Because life constantly adds and takes away, it is wise

never to measure your life's total worth by any single period in it. William Ernest Henley wrote the poem "Invictus" from his hospital bed. Although he had survived tuberculosis at age twelve, in the process, he had one foot amputated. He subsequently resisted the doctor's assurance that the only way to save his life was to amputate the other. As a result, Henley was discharged from the hospital in 1835 with one foot intact, and he went on to live and active life for thirty years despite his disability. This sort of belief in ourselves is where true victory begins. The things you think and say about yourself will always supersede the words spoken by others. You are truly the master of your fate and the captain of your soul.

You must also learn to enjoy your own company before you can enjoy the company of others. And for that, you need to be alone in order to evaluate your behavior, develop, improve, and grow. We all live in a world in which other people make constant demands on us, and as a consequence, we need time alone to sort through and evaluate the complexities of these relationships, and help us to get along better with others.

Self knowledge changes us. It is the vehicle that allows us to change our destiny. It gives us a new perspective thereby giving us a new point-of view. To change our destiny, we must first change ourselves.

## THE POWER OF ONE

*"I am only one, But still I am one." (Edward Everett Hale)*

One positive thought leads to another one. This is the power of one. Acknowledge that you have light within you. Your inner light will distinguish the true from the false and the good from the bad. Light illuminates. Light reveals. When you are a light unto yourself, you tap into the power of revelation. You become able to see what others fail to see, it is a gift from God. Some people call this gift "woman's intuition." Use this God-given talent to illuminate your path and raise the standard of what you will allow into your presence.

You cannot be a light for others until you are a light for yourself. The power of one requires you to elevate your inner light by raising your standards. "Neither do people light a lamp and put it under a bowl. Instead they put it on its stand, and it gives light to everyone in the house" (Matthew 5:15). Your stand and your standards are one. They are the rules by which you measure other things. Your standards signify what behaviors you will or will not accept so set them high and attract those who are your equal in expectations. Your power is in your inner light. The higher you raise the light, the greater the illumination causing everyone in your sphere to be illuminated. You will be able to see what others fail to see.

"The light of the body is the eye: if therefore thine eye be single, thy whole body shall be full of light" (Matthew 6:22 KJV). Harvest and concentrate your inner light by closing the window. The window, otherwise known as the eye or the lens, is the opening that allows the light to get in and out. The smaller you make the eye, the more concentrated and powerful the light becomes. In this context, I use the eye as an analogy for your intimate relationship. Be careful not to spread yourself too thin because, if you do, the less powerful you become. When you are intimate with someone, you give a part of yourself to them, and thus multiple relationships weaken you. Juggling them weakens you and your light.

The power of one is predicated on oneness with God. The

closer you are to God, the more light you will have to share with others. Allowing the light of God to shine on you helps you to improve. Light is most powerful at its origin. Light is brightest at its source. You are at the origin of the light within you. "The LORD is God, and he has made his light shine upon us" (Psalm 118:27). You are not the source, but you are the origin of the light. Just as the moon gets its light from the sun; your light comes from God. You are at the starting place because the source is within you. The closer you are to the light, the brighter the illumination.

Maximizing the power of one requires self-evaluation. Self-improvement is one of life's biggest challenges. In order to improve anything, you must first identify the problem as well as a solution, and then have the courage and discipline necessary to act. This requires that you to move close enough to the light to see the details involved, and that means more than just basking in the sun. What is necessary is the act of self-evaluation that lets the light shine directly on you, recognizing that the more you take in, the brighter the light will be. This additional illumination is your protection. It will keep you from stumbling in the dark. "Your word is a lamp to my feet and a light for my path." (Psalm 119:105). Before you can see man in a different light, you must first see your own pathway clearly.

## THE PRESENCE OF ONE

"God is light; in him there is no darkness at all" (1 John 1:5). Your time alone with God will allow you to discover the real power that is within you. Do not be afraid to be alone. You have the power to counter any attack the devil may make.

"Because the one who is in you is greater than the one who is in the world" (1 John 4:4). Look inwardly. The problem may be outside you, but the solution is on the inside. It is not by accident that your vital organs are protected within, particularly since your real treasures are in your heart.

Furthermore, your power begins and ends with you. Spend some of your time, energy, and talent doing things for yourself. This should not be an afterthought. It must be a priority, for if you give out more than you take in, you will lay waste to your power to be insightful. Often you must be alone in order to renew yourself, because you must come first in order to have the strength to help others. "For as he thinks in his heart, so is he" (Proverb 23:7 NKJV). Light shines on you when you are alone. The darkness that surrounds your sense of loneliness can become a weapon for any enemy that seeks to gain a stronghold in your life.

> "There is a tremendous difference between loneliness and aloneness. When you are lonely, you are thinking of the other, feeling that it would have been better if the other - your friend, your wife, your mother, your beloved, your husband – were there. Loneliness is absence of the other."
> Osho - *The Discipline of Transcendence Volume 1*, Chapter 2

Do not allow yourself to become lonely. Loneliness is a negative condition that equals you minus the other and it may also indicate that you place a greater importance on others than yourself. Loneliness suggests that you are less when others are not present. It makes you focus on them when you should be using your time alone to work on yourself. Relationship with others is a byproduct of "self," and as a consequence, strengthening yourself, strengthens your relationships. Shine the light inwardly and turn your loneliness into aloneness.

"Aloneness is the presence of oneself. Aloneness is very positive. It is a presence, overflowing presence. You are so full of presence that you can fill the whole universe with your presence and there is no need for anybody."
Osho - *The Discipline of Transcendence Volume 1*, Chapter 2

Aloneness is power. Aloneness is freedom. When there is no significant other, when there is quiet time, you have the power to develop yourself, to become greater than you are. All your energy, all your effort, the time and energy that you might otherwise have to expend on other people can be concentrated on yourself. Because of the power within you, you do not need anyone. "You will leave me all alone. Yet I am not alone, for my Father is with me" (John 16:32). Alone, everything in life can begin and end with you.

## POWER OF LIGHT

*You are the light of the world.*
*A city on a hill cannot be hidden.*
*(Mathew 5:14)*

Never live in the shadow of anyone. You have to determine this up front. Before and after any relationship, there will always be you. This is a powerful truth because you are full of power. You emit a light that cannot be hid, a light that illuminates your pathway and gives meaning to your journey. Others will be drawn to you, to your light. No darkness or sadness can overtake you when you let it shine. Rays of love will shine through the darkness, a signal of your strength and determination. You have the power within you to be a tower of light, a beacon for all to see.

Because you do not experience life alone, others will benefit from your successes. The light the moon gives off is a reflection of the light it gets from the sun. In just such a way, others will draw light from you. They will watch and imitate you. The choices and decisions you make serve as stepping stones for others to follow. You do not need to produce light to give light. You have the light of God within you. Let it shine!

Do not seek advice from others while ignoring the advice that comes from inside you for that advice is the best you can be given. Listen to your inner voice. God has given you an inherent scale of values to ensure that you will not be easily deceived. Nothing will help those who ignore their inner voice. Use this book to assist you in doing what your heart already knows you should do.

Many books have been written for the purpose of opening your eyes to others, but you must use the knowledge within you that illuminates you and your relationships. You need light to evaluate. Listen to the alarms that will warn you of pitfalls in your relationships. Learn from these alarms. They will not deceive you. They are a gift from God to keep you from being taken advantage of or deceived. These alarms are your protection. They will illuminate your situation.

To be full of light also means to be full of self-knowledge. People do the most harm to themselves when they lack the knowledge needed to change their current situations. Knowledge will show you how to attract those that will add to what you are, what you can be. When you shine the light on man, you shine the greatest light on yourself.

This book is divided into three parts, each dealing with ways to impact changes in your life. Part one deals with your relationships. Your words are your most powerful output. They are the gift others receive from you and are an external reflection of the inner you because they speak to what is in your heart. "For out of the overflow of the heart the mouth speaks" (Matthew 12:34). And it is not just what you say, but what you think as well. Thoughts can be seen as words not yet spoken. Negative thoughts lead to negative words. Your thoughts and words will shape what you receive so clearly state what you want.

Part two deals with your associations. Since men are of the earth, there are some whom you should avoid. Some people lift you up, while others pull you down. Just as you have to guard what you put out, you must also guard what you take in. Changing who you associate with changes your point of reference. Destination is a function of direction. Associations with people who are not heading in the direction that you are will take you off course. Your life is influenced by what you take it. Align the things that you take in with the destination you have in mind.

Finally, this book begins and ends with you. You have the most influence on your own life. The small changes you make inwardly produces exponential changes outwardly. Success in life is an external product of internal activity. You are the programmer. Every day your life runs on the internal program you create. Input determines output, output determines direction, and direction determines destiny. Changes to the inner you are the changes that will give you the real success you desire.

You are at the brink of greatness. There is a universe inside of you, and you have set on a journey of self-discovery. The launch is the most difficult part of any journey. It requires the most amount of energy, and you have just blasted off! The exploration has begun! All things begin and end with you! You have always been the light of the world, now you must be a light unto yourself!

## Chapter 2

# The War of the Emotions

You fight and war. (James 4:2 NKJV)

## COMPARABLE TO MAN

*"And the Lord said it is not good that man should be alone; I will make him a helper comparable to him."*
*(Genesis 2:18 NKJV)*

You cannot have a conversation about men without talking about relationships. The interactions between man and woman will always be one of life's biggest challenges, and yet half of all marriages presently end in divorce. The stats are no different for Christian marriages than from any other, probably because men and women customarily approach relationship from two different points of reference. Adam was created alone, and Eve was created in a relationship. Man was created first therefore; he was comfortable being alone. Adam had no real concept of relationship until God instructed him to name all the animals. Only then did Adam realize that he alone had no one like himself to turn to. It was a defining moment.

Unlike Adam, Eve was created in a relationship so it was natural for her to be in one from the beginning. She came from man, therefore she was emotionally comparable to him. "She shall be call woman because she was taken out of man" (Genesis 2:23 NKJV). Woman is the part of man with which he longs to reconnect. She knows what he needs even without him saying it. Man's basic desire is to be united with her as one flesh, and this desire supersedes all others. "Therefore shall a man leave his father and his mother and be joined unto his wife and they shall be one flesh" (Genesis 2:24 NKJV).

Although woman is comparable to man, man is *not* comparable to woman. There is nothing on earth that compares to her. After God created Adam, he took one of his ribs to create Eve. Woman was twice in the Master Designer's hand. No other creature on earth can make that claim. She is the mother of all things and life begins in her womb. Although she is part of his basic design, he is not part of hers. God took a part of Adam's flesh and created something to which nothing can compare.

When God created woman, she was complete and entire. She had everything she needed internally and externally to be whole. Woman understands man because she came from him. She was once inside of him, and she knows him from the inside out. She is bone of his bone and flesh of his flesh, and coming as she does from man, she naturally understands his needs, and can be his helpmate. It is not good for man to be alone. God created woman from one of his ribs to take away his loneliness.

## THE BATTLE WITHIN

*Where do wars and fights come from among you?*
*(James 4:1 NKJV)*

If God created woman for man, why do these two sexes so often war with one another? Where do these conflicts begin? All wars, beginning as they do from within, creates external battles. The battle without is generated from the battle within. Understanding the inner workings of man helps to make sense of the outer struggle.

Man came from the earth and was an empty shell before God breathed life into him. This emptiness is still a part of his emotional makeup. It gives him the capacity to wage war and still go home and make love to his wife. Man is has within him an empty shell which makes it possible for him to deaden his emotions, leaving him able to deal dispassionately with the consequences of his actions. Man has within him the ability to suppress his emotions.

Unlike man, woman, who was not fashioned as he from the earth, is an emotional being. God created woman with the ability to bring forth life. She is able to sense the subtle changes of a child growing in her womb. Woman is connected to the child physically and emotionally simply because she was designed to bear offspring, to nurture, and care for them. It is her nature to love and to show emotions. Because woman was created in a relationship with man from the beginning, it is natural for her to be in one.

There is a little doubt that men and women are engaged in a war of emotions due to the fact that men's emotions are limited and women's are limitless. Relatively speaking, if a man has five emotional strings, then a woman has five thousand, an imbalance that makes conflict inevitable. Many battles begin because man is so uncomfortable with his emotions that he avoids confrontations that might involve them. If he tries to contend, he is usually no match for a woman. The battle usually ends when the man maneuvers the situation in such a way that he is no longer called on to feel, leaving him free to move on to the next thing. The woman is then left alone to deal with her emotions.

Struggles involving emotion damage relationships. Most men do not like to lose at anything, and if they find themselves losing the battle emotionally, they will try to make it a battle of words which can be harsh and damaging. If he continues to lose, man may resort to violence which, in turn, causes him more internal conflict. Because man has an empty shell, emotionally, he is able to put his violent episodes into that temporary storage place, leaving the woman alone again to deal with her feelings. This often becomes a pattern of behavior, with the same basic outcomes.

The fallout of emotional warfare is frequently devastating, leaving men emotionally numb and women emotionally scarred, creating a void in communication and destroying intimacy. Relationships are visibly damaged by these types of emotional battles. The hidden danger is that they may also result in a desire in both men and women to seek love and peace in all the wrong places, with the unfortunate result that they often go on to wound others in the same ways they have been hurt.

However, the loss of a single battle does mean the war is lost. Although man is limited in his ability to cope with emotions, he is not without them. To understand this, you must go below the surface to the place where his real emotions reside. The definition of emotion comes from the Middle French word *emouvior which* means "to stir up." Just so, your quest to understand man must take you below the surface. I do not say this lightly. I know digging below the surface will be painful. Whenever nerves are exposed, they become sensitive to everything. This process will cause pain, but it is necessary for permanent healing to take place. Stay the course, and you will be better in end.

The battle involved in establishing a lasting relationship begins within. Man has an internal longing for woman, but this longing is spiritual as much as it is physical. Man is constantly trying to reconnect with the part of himself that God used to create woman. Some men try to do this without the complexity of being in a committed relationship. Many men believe they can resolve this conflict by merely sleeping with women.

When a man is intimate with a woman, he becomes one flesh with her and temporarily feels complete. He enters her body and leaves a part of himself within her. This physical oneness serves as a temporary substitute for spiritual oneness; something that, ironically enough, the woman needs in order for a physical union to make her feel complete. This physical, emotional, and spiritual mismatch is a major part of the war of emotions.

## BRIDGE OVER TROUBLED EMOTIONS

The war of the emotions will never be resolved with a war of words. Common ground must be reached before treaties can be forged. Communication aimed at winning the battle while losing the other person will only work to further the divide. Over time, this great divide will appear as a span between the man and woman that cannot be crossed. When this happens, real effective communications is needed to bring a couple to a common ground of understanding and trust. When couples find common ground, they are on the way to putting an end to emotional warfare. Of course, this will not happen unless both parties are working together to make it happen, both willing to put in the time and effort needed to make the relationship work.

Wars are ended with treaties. A treaty is an agreement or arrangement reached via negotiations which represent a meeting of the minds. When the parties involved come together at the negotiation table, the lines of communication are opened, the ability to resolve the issue becomes possible, and the bridge over troubled emotions is brought to the forefront.

Words and actions that work for the good of the relationship are the foundations for establishing common ground. Honest communication about one's thoughts and feelings that are clearly communicated and respectfully received will serve as the bridge over trouble emotions. We cannot allow relationships and marriages to end simply because it is a lot of work to maintain them. There is too much at stake.

There is no force more powerful in this world that a man and woman working together. Their union creates families, generations, countries, worlds and universes. When a man and woman are united in love, the whole world pauses and takes notice, and a new world comes into being. Together they are able to bring forth life. It follows; therefore, that the pursuit of this oneness is the greatest of all endeavors. When it is achieved, it becomes a model, compass, and roadmap for others to follow.

# Chapter 3

# The Whole Truth

*I am telling you nothing but the truth (Job 36:4)*

## THE BATTLE FOR THE TRUTH

*"...who desires all men to be saved and to come to the knowledge of the truth" (1 Timothy 2:4)*

"THEN David sent messengers to get her. She came to him, and he slept with her. (She had purified herself from her uncleanness.) Then she went back home" (2 Samuel 11: 4). The desire that a man has to sleep with a woman does not necessarily translate into a desire to want to commit to her. King David saw Bathsheba bathing, and sent for her to come to him. What David did not say was that he had a hidden agenda, a desire to sleep with her. Real truth often lives below the surface.

Commitment is not automatic. David's slept with Bathsheba and sent her back home. As far as he was concerned, the relationship was over. His actions spoke to his true intentions. A man may say that you are beautiful, and that he wants to marry you, but does he have a ring? Is he willing to set a date? Beware of words without actions. Actions reveal more about a man than words alone ever could. The battle for the truth begins with a man's actions.

Words alone cannot be the measure of intentions. Motives are important too, since often there are hidden agendas to be taken into consideration. Words support our actions, but words cannot replace them. When there is a conflict between our words and our actions, our actions supersede our words. It is important not to be so emotional involved in a relationship that you believe whatever you hear even when there are no actions that support those words. Compare words to actions. This is how you evaluate truth. Actions that support a man's words reveal his intentions. The truth is revealed through words and deeds. This is where your freedom lives. "And you shall know the truth and the truth shall make you free" (John 8:32 NKJV).

The power of words is dependent on who is speaking. David used his position as king to give his words power. When a king speaks, his words have more power than those of an ordinary person. David's intention was to sleep with Bathsheba. He inquired about her, sent for her, and slept with her. He may have told her she was beautiful, but his intent was to take her to his bed. When a woman relies on a man's words, regardless of his actions, she embraces a surface truth. This is dangerous ground because most men will not own up to their actions until they are faced with the consequences of them.

## CONSEQUENCES BRING FORTH EMOTIONS

All actions have consequences. Certainly David was later confronted with the negative consequences of his. After he slept with Bathsheba, she became pregnant. He tried to cover up his mistake by sending for her husband, but Uriah refused to return from his commitment to war to join his wife. To make matters worse, David sent Uriah off to battle and ensured that he was killed.

David thought he had successfully managed to disguise the truth until Nathan the prophet told David a story about a man who took a lamb from his neighbor's sheepfold, even though he had many sheep and lambs of his own. He took from another what he already had in his possession. When David heard the story, he became enraged and declared that any man that did such a thing should be put to death!

David was devastated when Nathan's response was to tell him, "Thou art the man!" Consequences bring forth emotions. David showed no emotions when he slept with Bathsheba. He showed no emotions when he had Uriah killed, but when he was confronted with the consequences of his actions, he surrendered to sorrow, and wrote Psalms 51, asking God for forgiveness. He pleaded with God begging him to cleanse his heart and renew his spirit.

Like David, when a man is confronted with his actions, his emotions may range from remorse to anger, depending on the man. Some men are so uncomfortable with their emotions that they will try to hide them. This lack of emotional responsibility leaves everyone involved in the dark. Nevertheless, these hidden emotions are a part of the struggles that follow.

# KNOW THE TRUTH

Every action, whether seen or unseen, creates a reaction. Nathan confronted King David with the knowledge of what he had done. He wanted David, in turn, to confront the unseen results of his actions. Nathan proved that it is possible to confront without being confrontational by stressing knowledge of the sort gained by asking question. Even if these go unanswered, something can be learned since what is not said can be as powerful as what is said.

The things that really matter in relationships often cannot be seen with the naked eye. Each woman should conduct her own survey, checking out contour of the land. Make sure the man you are considering involving yourself with is mentally and physically healthy. Also make sure that he is financially stable, single and available. Don't assume anything. Remember that the basis for real knowledge is often just below surface. Allow time to take you below what we call "surface knowledge."

How do you go below the surface in search of the truth? First, evaluate the other types of relationship he has had with the other women in his life. Start with his relationship with his mother, as well as his other female relations. This information will shine additional light on the type of man you are dealing with. Evaluate it dispassionately. When emotions are involved, logic goes out the window. Every day you are given bits and pieces of information, none of which you should ignore. This is your key to gaining knowledge without confrontation. Asking the right questions before you are emotionally involved will help you to avoid a lot of headaches and heartaches down the road.

# MAN-TALK

*Love does not delight in evil but rejoices with the truth (1 Corinthians 13:6)*

There is an old story about two people named Truth and Lie. One hot day, Truth decided to take a swim. Having nothing to swim in, he removed his clothing and jumped in the water in his birthday suit. Lie came along and seeing Truth's clothing on the bank decided to put them on and head into town. When Truth got out the water and realized what had happened, he followed Lie, stark naked. When the people in town saw them coming, they cried out, "Look at Lie all dressed up like the Truth, and look at Truth coming in behind him naked as can be." The moral of the story is that no matter how you dress up a lie, it is still a lie, and no matter how naked the truth is, it is still the truth.

Men have their own version of the truth, usually based on logic. If there is any danger of emotion entering the picture, men will battle to keep it in check. I remember that, even as a little boy, I would tell myself not to cry because it was a sign of weakness. Emotions were a luxury I could not afford to have. For a man, the battle against showing emotions begins long before he comes into contact with a woman. Because of this, men are often oblivious when it comes to the long term emotional damage their words may create.

Most men use words primarily to obtain information or to gain the advantage that comes with knowing more about the woman than she does about him. Although no man will admit to this, he feels empowered by keeping you in the dark. This results in coded "man-talk," which includes answering questions truthfully without really saying anything. For example, if you were to ask the question, "Where have you been?" his response might simply be that he has been "out with the boys." He has answered the question truthfully, but without giving you any significant information, after which he may counter the question with one of his own. Even if you are successful at getting any information, "man-talk" may make that process as painful as pulling teeth. Once the conversation is finally over, the woman will most likely have given out more revealing information then she gained.

Some men will use the knowledge they acquire to take advantage of women. Having watched Bathsheba bathing on the roof, seeing her naked beauty and sensing her loneliness, David inquired. "Who is she? Is she married? Where is her husband?" Every piece of information he received about her made her more vulnerable to his power, leaving Bathsheba at a real disadvantage. Despite the fact that David was the king, she knew little about him and this lack of knowledge left her emotionally exposed. Her questions, unlike his, were probably simple responses to his command. "Why is he sending for me? What am I to say? How should I act?" A woman is emotionally naked when she has no knowledge of a man's intentions. This one-sided exchange is "man-talk" at its greatest.

Knowledge empowers a woman. This goes beyond surface knowledge. When a woman knows a man's intentions, she becomes powerful. "My people are destroyed from lack of knowledge" (Hosea 4:6). A lack of knowledge is very dangerous. Knowledge is its own reward because it leads to the truth.

Although words are connected to truth, they are not truth. Words carry knowledge, but they also convey emotions. Truth stands alone. It does not need emotions to support it. "Then you will know the truth, and the truth will set you free" (John 8:32). Only the truth you know will free you. Without this knowledge, you will be forced to wait for the truth to reveal itself. Seek out truth. You can never be truly free without it.

Always keep in mind the fact that some words work against reality. They need not be outright lies. They can be a twisted version of the truth, shrouded in fake emotions. These words sound like truth, but have nothing concrete to support them because they only live by virtue of having been spoken. And this is particularly dangerous because, although you would discount a lie immediately, words shrouded by distortions keep you lingering and listening, a captive to these half-truths.

It is only the truth you know that can ever free you. The truth you don't know does you no good. Just because someone is not lying, does not mean they are honest. They could be merely keeping the real truth to themselves. Real truth comes from real intentions of the heart that are expressed with honesty and sincerity.

The war of words and truth is a subset of the war of the emotions. They both work against relationships putting a gulf between the two people involved. This gulf will only widen over time. It will magnify the emotional difference between men and women and give power to emotional warfare. If this war is allowed to continue, relationships will die. Only open, honest, heart-felt communication can serve as a bridge over troubled emotions.

Not all men are honest. The next few chapters will deal with the ways men damage relationships through immaturity, cheating and neglect. These behaviors work against relationships and worsen the war of the emotions. The more truth you know about these men, the less impact they will have. The truth you don't know does you no good, but the truth you know sets you free.

## Chapter 4

# Why do Men Cheat?

*Anyone who can be trusted in little matters can also be trusted in important matters. But anyone who is dishonest in little matters will be dishonest in important matters (Luke 16:10 CEV)*

### THE HEART FACTOR

BEFORE I begin to discuss the subject of why men cheat, I must first address one of the aftermath of cheating. Cheating, like death and war, takes no prisoners, leaving whomever it touches, including families, neighborhoods, and communities devastated. The church, work environment, and family structure are all also impacted. Cheating tears at the fabric of our society, and diminishes the heart and creativity of the injured person. Wounded men and women are teaching our kids, cooking our food, driving our school busses, and flying our planes. Whether intentional, or unintentional, unfaithfulness creates a battleground within the relationship. The war of the emotions can never be ended as long as infidelity occurs. When relationships suffer, we are all lessened in some way.

Since men who are unfaithful inflict serious damage to their relationships, why would a man ever cheat? Although there is no single answer to this all important question, I believe there are some common threads that tear at the fabric of relationships. The most important of all of these threads is the conditions of a man's heart. "For out of the overflow of the heart the mouth speaks. The good man brings good things out of the good stored up in him, and the evil man brings evil things out of the evil stored up in him" (Mathew 12:34, 35).

Cheating comes from the heart. Men that are unfaithful act out what is in their heart. You cannot make a man cheat. Cheating is the symptom. It reflects the spiritual condition of the heart. "For out of the heart come evil thoughts, murder, adultery, sexual immorality, theft, false testimony, slander" (Mathew 15:19). Internal desire determines external behavior. It is not what is outside a man that defiles his heart. "Do you not understand that whatever goes into the man from outside cannot defile him" (Mark 7:18 NASB). What is in a man's heart will determine his course of actions. His biggest problems are within him.

Men have often blamed their wives or girlfriends for their unfaithfulness, citing such excuses as, "She doesn't satisfy me sexually anymore," or "She has gained too much weight." They try to lead us to believe that the source their problem is outside of them. But these excuses are just covers to justify their actions. A man does not cheat because of someone else or simply because he thinks he can get away with it. He could choose to throw himself off the roof, but he does not because he knows that he will not like the consequences. A man cheats because it is in his heart to do it.

A man with a cheating heart will cheat regardless of whom

he is with. He is not unfaithful because he has no other choice. On the contrary, he is unfaithful because he chooses to be. After all, he has within him the power to say no, to walk away, or to choose some other course of action. If adultery is in a man's heart, he is destined to be unfaithful. "For from within, out of men's hearts, come evil thoughts, sexual immorality, theft, murder, adultery," (Mark 7:21). Webster's dictionary defines adultery as voluntary sexual intercourse between a married person and someone other than their spouse. The heart will be the determining factor. Spiritual insight alone, rather than conventional wisdom can reveal the desires of the heart.

## THE DESIRE FACTOR

What is in a man's heart will determine his desires. When the word of God is in his heart, he will desire the word. "I have hidden your word in my heart that I might not sin against you" (Psalm 119:11). When lust is in a man's heart he will desire that which alone can satisfy it. "But every man is tempted, when he is drawn away of his own lust, and enticed" (James 1:14 KJV). This is what happened when David, long before he became "a man after God own heart," (Acts 13:22), lusted after Bathsheba. Seeing her naked, he no longer considered the consequences of his action. David knew what was in his heart was wrong, but he did not stop to use his reason. He saw her! He desired her! He took her! David was so taken with Bathsheba that he never considered his other choices.

David is not alone. All men have two natures. An external nature that desires what it sees, and a spiritual nature that desires what is in his heart. "Those who live according to the sinful nature have their minds set on what that nature desires; but those who live in accordance with the Spirit have their minds set on what the Spirit desires" (Romans 8:5).

In Genesis 12:10-20, we find the story of Abram and Sarai his wife. Before they entered into the city, Abram told Sarai to tell the Egyptians she was his sister and not his wife. He believed that because of her beauty, the Egyptians would kill him to get to her. He was certain that the partial truth, that she was his half-sister would somehow save his life. Abram understood the nature of men who desire what they see.

When the princes of Egypt saw Sarai and realized how beautiful she was, they commanded her to be brought before Pharaoh, and he was so taken by her beauty, thinking she was single and available, showered Abram with riches. "He treated Abram well for her sake, and Abram acquired sheep and cattle, male and female donkeys, menservants and maidservants, and camels" (Genesis 12:15, 16).

Pharaoh did not hide the fact that he desired Sarai, showering her with attention and praise. Had God not intervened, Pharaoh would have taken Abram's wife for himself. It was only because he feared God's punishment that Pharaoh sent Abram and Sarai out of his country along with the gifts and servants that he gave to Abram for her sake.

The desire that is in a man's heart will manifest itself in external behavior. He will do what is in his heart to do, but you cannot look into a man's heart to determine its spiritual condition. You can only look at what comes out of it. Observe a man's actions, and they will give you spiritual insight. Lying, cheating, and stealing are generated from the same heart as adultery. These things are just as much of a sign of unfaithfulness as adultery itself.

A man will cheat because he desires what he sees and acts on this desire. Cheating begins in a man's heart and is later manifest in his actions because cheating is a function of the heart. "But I tell you that anyone who looks at a woman lustfully has already committed adultery with her in his heart" (Mathew 5:28).

## THE VISUAL FACTOR

Although what a man sees cannot make him cheat unless it is in his heart to do so, it can give him pause. Women's sexuality has distracted men since the beginning of time. Just as advertisers today use women's sexuality to get men to buy their products, spies use women to obtain secrets from powerful men. They both bank on the fact that a man will respond to what he sees. Some men will give almost anything to get what they want from women. When the daughter of Herodias danced for King Herod, he was so taken with her that he was willing to give her whatever she wanted, even up to half his kingdom (Matt. 14:6, 7). Her mother Herodias used her to get the head of John the Baptist (Matt. 14:8). Because of visual temptation, men may cease to reason, to act without thinking, thus uncontrolled desires bring mighty men to their knees.

A man's status does not exempt him from consequences. "On Herod's birthday, the daughter of Herodias danced for them and pleased Herod so much that he promised with an oath to give her whatever she asked. Prompted by her mother, she said, "give me here on a platter the head of John the Baptist.' The king was distressed, but because of the oaths he had made before his dinner guests, he ordered that her request be granted" (Mathew 14:6-9). King Herod became a victim of his desires. Every man must accept the consensuses of his actions. "Do not be deceived: God cannot be mocked. A man reaps what he sows. The one who sows to please his sinful nature, from that nature will reap destruction; the one who sows to please the Spirit, from the Spirit will reap eternal life" (Galatians 6:7-8).

When a man can no longer control his desires, he becomes their servant. The Philistines were no match for Samson, but Samson was no match for the women in his life. The Philistine used his wife to get the answer to a riddle about a lion's carcass filled with honey that caused Samson to lose a bet with the Philistines. This bet was the beginning of trouble between Samson and the Philistine (Judges 14:17). They used Delilah to find out the secret to his strength (Judges 16:17, 18). Samson was an unbeatable foe whose desires became his downfall. Men who are in control of their desires will rule over those who are not. Samson lack of control cost him his eyes and his life. Uncontrolled desires can have deadly consequences.

What a man sees distract him from logic, and this will have consequences. Because of such a distraction, Adam was put out of the garden, never to return again. Just so, many men will never get a second chance to correct the errors of their ways. Their actions may cost them their families, careers, relationships, and lives. The news today is full of men making bad choices. All too many men have fallen prey to their visual desires. These men were victims of "thoughts interrupted."

Each man is responsible for his own actions. He cannot blame others for his lack of control. Adam found this out. He tried to blame Eve, but God held him responsible. To Adam he said, “Because you listened to your wife and ate from the tree about which I commanded you, 'You must not eat of it,' "Cursed is the ground because of you; through painful toil you will eat of it all the days of your life” (Genesis 3:17). The expulsion from the garden was collateral damage of thoughts interrupted by visual desires its worst.

## FRIENDLY FIRE

Another form of collateral damage caused by lust is friendly fire. I refer to cheating as “friendly-fire,” a term that I use to describe a situation in which someone that is on your side, someone that is suppose to be there to protect you, causes you harm. Friendly-fire can be deadly. The most grievous of all friendly-fire is infidelity. When men are unfaithful, they cause harm to the very person they should be protecting. These wounds cut deep into the heart of the woman. Friendly-fire cause emotional damage as well. It leaves women wondering how anyone who was supposed to protect them could hurt them so badly. They find themselves asking, how could he be so careless, and how could he be so selfish.

Infidelity is friendly-fire as its worst, and the wounds it incurs must be treated immediately because, whatever the condition may be, it will only get worse over time. No hurt can go untreated. No wound can go uncovered. What actions should be taken if the bomb of infidelity blows up in your relationships? What steps should be taken to keep friendly-fire from turning deadly? Here are three steps that have spiritual as well as practical application.

Step one, stop the bleeding. Cheating creates an explosive situation that, in turn, creates an emotional battlefield. This is not the time for the wounded to continue the battle. There are those who will want to get right back into the fray or go on as if the infidelity has not occurred. Some will try to keep the incident a secret to protect their spouse, but a cover-up is never a good idea. The wounded person is the one that needs the care. Infidelity causes a wound in the heart that may be accompanied with internal bleeding which, because of its very nature, must be stopped. The wounded should not be allowed to care for themselves. Never leave emotional healing to chance. There are trusted people in everyone's circle who are qualified to provide spiritual and emotional support.

The second step is to protect the wound. Healing is never instantaneous. It takes time to recover from a broken heart. Be careful not to allow the person that wounded you to continue to hurt you. Place a bandage over your heart until it heals. Allow the word of God to begin to work on you. The damage may have cut deeper than ever imagined. Spiritual and emotional scaring may have occurred.

At the same time, life goes on, and most people do not have the luxury of living in the recovery room. We are all exposed to the elements and the scrutiny of public opinion. Whenever an injury occurs, everyone wants to see what it looks like. They will ask you to expose your scares for the benefit of their viewing. This will involve reliving the horror of what happen over and over again. I recommend that only those that are providing care be allowed access to your wounded heart. Keep all emotional wounds covered and protected, and only let qualified professional remove the emotional bandages.

Lastly, the shock should be treated. This requires as immediate action as it would on an actual battlefield when clothing is loosened, and feet are elevated. One of the most effective treatments for the sort of shock which follows the discovery of adultery is to be found in the words of the caregiver who must remain calm and provide comfort. Letting a person know that they will recover gives them the strength they need to endure. Words are medicine. Words are life.

## THE SPIRITUAL FACTOR

There is help for the cheating heart. A man's response to the word of God is a direct reflection of the condition of his heart. If God's word is in his heart, it will agree with the word that he hears, and his actions will coincide with the word of God. If the word of God is not in a man's heart, he will reject what he hears, and his actions will be contrary to what he has heard. Imprinting the word of God on a man's heart will help to change his desires. And since man's external desire is a byproduct of what is stored internally, when a man hears the word of God, his response determines the spiritual conditions of his heart. This invisible response speaks volume about the man. You need spiritual insight to tap into this knowledge.

X-ray machines allow us to see inside the human body so that doctors can diagnose diseases, the symptoms of which might otherwise have been attributed to something external like an adverse reaction to something the patient ate. Before the invention of the x-ray machine, many died never knowing the real causes of their problems, some of which could have been successfully treated if they had been discovered in time. Without the aid of the x-ray machine, the root cause of many of man's problems went undiscovered. Although the invention of the x-ray machine is a thing of the past, there is still no machine to let us see into the spirit of man. To look there, spiritual insight is needed, insight which can illuminate the moral condition of a man's heart. Spiritual insight comes from the word of God.

Some men have good intentions in their heart. Joseph refused to compromise his relationship with God by accepting the advances of Potiphar's wife. "And though she spoke to Joseph day after day, he refused to go to bed with her or even be with her. One day he went into the house to attend to his duties, and none of the household servants were inside. She caught him by his cloak and said, 'Come to bed with me!' But he left his cloak in her hand and ran out of the house" (Genesis 39:10-12). Joseph refused to sleep with Potiphar's wife despite her literally ripping his clothes off his body. Refusing her advances caused him to be unjustly imprisoned, but he maintained his integrity which came for the good that was stored in Joseph's heart.

Faithfulness is a function of the heart. Man will never get to the source of what is really ailing him without evaluating his relationship with God. If the problem is spiritual in nature then the solution must be spiritual as well. "For if you live according to the sinful nature, you will die; but if by the Spirit you put to death the misdeeds of the body, you will live," (Romans 8:13).

Man's biggest problems are spiritual in nature, and they are directly related to his relationship with God. Infidelity comes from within. God looks at the heart of man (1 Samuel 16:7). Man's heart is where the problem resides (Matthew 15:19), and it is where the solution must be found. "So then, those who are in the flesh cannot please God" (Romans 8:8). Cheating is an external problem with an internal spiritual origin. You will need spiritual insight to see the real source of man's problem.

Unfaithfulness begins in the heart of man. "Out of your heart come evil thoughts, murder, unfaithfulness in marriage, (Matthew 15:19 CEV).

A man cheats because his heart follows the patterns of this world and it has not been transformed, therefore, you are neither the problem nor the solution. "Create in me a clean heart, O God; and renew a right spirit within me" (Psalm 51:10 KJV). Each man must give an account for his own action. He must present himself to God. Cheating is an internal problem that requires an internal spiritual solution.

"Therefore, I urge you, brothers, in view of God's mercy, to offer your bodies as living sacrifices, holy and pleasing to God—this is your spiritual act of worship. Do not conform any longer to the pattern of this world, but be transformed by the renewing of your mind. Then you will be able to test and approve what God's will is—his good, pleasing and perfect will" (Romans 12:1-2). Because unfaithfulness begins in the heart of man, the only real help will be through him allowing God to renew his heart. This is his responsibility.

## CHAPTER 5

# The Danger of a Neglected Woman

*May your fountain be blessed, and may you rejoice in the wife of your youth.*
*(Proverbs 5:18)*

## VALUE OF A WIFE

*He who finds a wife finds what is good and receives favor from the LORD.*
*(Proverbs 18:22)*

**EVERY** man should be happy to be married for his wife is the most important relationship he will ever have. This highest level of commitment two people can make to one another can be a fountain of blessing. Because of that, this chapter's purpose is to provide an insight into the necessity of an examination of the marriage state, no matter how painful it may be. Like the skillful hand of a surgeon, the word of God cuts away anything this is contrary to your growth and development. The scriptural insight you receive from the word of

God is spiritual insight you can live by. This chapter speaks of God's voice, and it will help you to find your own. "I treasure your word above all else; it keeps me from sinning against you" (Psalms 119:11CEV).

A wife's words are man's emotional compass. She should use them to help keep him from drifting off course. They are the caution lights and the flashing signals that will alert him that he is about to wander off the path. A wife should be able to share her needs and desires with her husband. If he treasures her, her words end up in his heart, the only place he has to store his emotional treasures. These words will help keep him from losing his way back to her.

Some men, having lost their sense of commitment, must struggle to find their way home. Perhaps they have sought to replace what comes straight from the heart with that which comes from the hand. Many believe houses, cars, boats, jewelry, and credit cards will satisfy a woman's desire for a committed relationship. And in order to understand that this is not enough, they must be told. Saying what you want does not make you needy or high maintenance. It makes you valuable because it is your words that will lead a man to the treasures of your heart. This is where the real you resides. This is where he will reap the harvest of blessings. The right words will yield the right harvest.

Because the responsibility is so great, women should choose their words carefully. They should also keep in mind the fact that what they say is bound to be a reflection of how they are feeling at that time. In doing so, they may be limiting themselves to speaking only in the "present tense," addressing only what a man is and not what he can become. Actions speak louder, but words are more powerful. Words precede actions. Words create actions; they shape relationships. The words of a wife helps man to better understand and appreciate her value to him.

## VALUE OF WORDS

Don't worry about addressing the 'now.' Words are powerful enough to counter what is in the present tense. Words set into motions what can be. Learn to speak through your spirit, using God's words as the catalyst that enables your words to reach the heart of man.

Words spoken through your spirit are powerful. They are not based on how you feel. Your feelings feed on someone else's actions, but your spirit feeds on the word of God. Speak God's words and give power to your words. "For the word of God is quick, and powerful, and sharper than any two-edged sword" (Hebrews 4:12 KJV). When you speak God's words, you overpower the now with what can be.

God's words are valuable because they speak positively about relationships. They tell us that a man should cleave to his wife, thus demonstrating that he places the highest value on that relationship. This also shows that he intends to give his wife the attention she deserves, as a way of demonstrating that she has value to him. If a man neglects his wife, hoping to make up for this with gifts, it is clear that she is not in his heart which is where we store everything we truly value. Neglect tells a woman that she has little value to her husband, and it may be an indicator of the fact that something or someone else may be his heart's priority.

The sad truth is that some men will never know how valuable their wives are until they have lost them. These are men who have never learned to trust their inner judgment. They always need someone else to tell them the value of what they possess. This is true for their relationships as well. These men often seem to value the relationship more once it is over. They spend more time, energy, and money trying to get back into a relationship then they ever did when they were in it. They failed to see the woman's worth until it was too late.

## TRUE VALUE

*I praise you because I am fearfully and wonderfully made;*

*(Psalm 139:14)*

When a man finds a wife, she comes to him as a favor from God. If he chooses to let her go, it does not mean that she was not worth keeping; he has simply failed to see the value of what he had. God has declared the wife to be fearfully and wonderfully made, always more than what others are able to see, just as every woman is uniquely created by God. Some men may never see the true value that you, as a woman, have to offer. Learn to see in yourself what others fail to see. This is one of the many steps towards self-discovery, a roadmap for others. Many men need this map to understand the true value that each woman has to offer.

True value begins with the individual and is transcended by those who are around them. Some people add to us, while others take away. Some women attach themselves to men who constantly put them down, creating in themselves a reflection of a negative image. Others, more fortunate, become close to men who see them as more than they are, making it easy for them to reflect this positive image. How a man sees a woman influences how she sees herself. When a man sees value in a woman, he treats her differently and ultimately she becomes different. It is very important for men to see the value of their wives. If not, someone else may well recognize what he fails to see.

## MISPLACED VALUES

*Then David said to Uriah, "Go down to your house and wash your feet." So Uriah left the palace, and a gift from the king was sent after him. But Uriah slept at the entrance to the palace with all his master's servants and did not go down to his house (2 Samuel 11:8, 9)*

Dangerous things happen when a husband fails to see the value of his wife. David was the King of Israel, and Bathsheba was the wife of Uriah, a soldier in his army. The story line in the Bible focuses mainly on David and his affair with the married Bathsheba, but there is another *story line*. In the verses above, David instructs Uriah to go home to his wife, but Uriah refuses to go feeling it would have be disloyal to his troops. In doing so, he neglected not only his wife, but also his duties as a husband, choosing instead to sleep on the porch with David's servants. Uriah misplaced view of loyalty and commitment cause him to fail to see that he had a responsibility and loyalty to his wife first and foremost.

In the end, David saw in Bathsheba what her husband did not. "And from the roof he saw a woman washing herself; and the woman was very beautiful to look upon" (2 Samuel 11:2

KJV). He sent for her, and after Uriah's death, made her his wife, preferring her above all the women in Israel. From her loins came Solomon, the greatest of all the kings of Israel.

Be aware that men today often make this same mistake. They get caught in the hustle and bustle of their life, focusing on everything except their wives, making them a secondary priority. This is a dangerous mistake. Men must make their wives their first priority, and everything else will find its proper place in their lives.

Like Uriah, some men have a tendency to focus single-mindedly on things outside of the relationship, leaving the women in their lives feeling neglected. This neglect may be unintentional, but it still hurts. Although people can be neglected physically, emotionally, or spiritually, emotional neglect is the most subtle of the three. More and more married women are finding themselves alone emotionally. Out of sight, out of mind seems to be the theme of the time.

Sight is important to men because they desire what they see. When a man loses sight of the most significant relationship in his life, he opens the door for trouble. Neglect is defined by *Webster's dictionary* as to give little attention or respect, or to leave undone or unattended especially through carelessness. Webster further states that neglect implies giving insufficient attention to something that merits one's attention. Neglect inevitably has negative consequences, often resulting in separation, and the sort of loss that Uriah experienced after he did not give Bathsheba the attention she deserved. She was not in his view because his focus was on the war and his desire followed his focus.

## VALUE OF SIGHT

*Late one afternoon, after his midday rest, David got out of bed and was walking on the roof of the palace. As he looked out over the city, he noticed a woman of unusual beauty taking a bath. He sent someone to find out who she was, and he was told, "She is Bathsheba, the daughter of Eliam and the wife of Uriah the Hittite."*
*(2 Sam 11:2-3 NLT)*

David noticed Bathsheba. She was in his view. He did not know who she was until he saw her, but when he saw her, he desired her. This was the beginning of trouble. After sending for Bathsheba, David slept with her and she became pregnant. More trouble followed. To cover his tracks, David summoned Uriah and tried to send him home, but Uriah refused because he was, at that moment, thinking of nothing except the war.

Bathsheba was not in Uriah sight. A wife provides her husband with his most valuable relationship. She is more valuable than his career, ministry, military service, or call to duty. We can applaud Uriah as a solider, but we should be disappointed in him as a husband. He should have gone home. His wife was his first priority. "When a man hath taken a new wife, he shall not go out to war, neither shall he be charged with any business: but he shall be free at home one year, and shall cheer up his wife which he has taken" (Deuteronomy 24:5).

Uriah priorities were out of order, as he said when he indicated that his heart was with the troops. Uriah spoke of the Ark, Israel, the troops, and Joab, but Bathsheba was last on the list. He was more concerned about the captain of the army then he was for his wife. Bathsheba should have been his first priority and he should have valued her as a part of him. "So ought men to love their wives as their own bodies" (Eph 5:28 KJV).

By making Bathsheba the least of his priorities, Uriah quite literally lost sight of her. She was a part of him and she should have been at the forefront of his mind. What a man says tells us what is on his mind. If men list their jobs before their families, something is wrong with their thought process. "You are snared by the words of your mouth" (Proverbs 6:2 NKJV).

"Uriah said to David, the ark and Israel and Judah are staying in tents, and my master Joab and my lord's men are camped in the open fields. How could I go to my house to eat and drink and lie with my wife? As surely as you live, I will not do such a thing!" (2 Samuel 11:11). With the single statement, Uriah established the value of his relationship with his wife, since he mentioned her last. His mind and heart were elsewhere. He made a decision not to go home without knowing what was happening there. He spoke out of ignorance, and his actions followed his words.

Uriah's refusal to go home was a form of spiritual, emotional and physical neglect. It was spiritual neglect because Uriah was Bathsheba's husband and spiritually they were one flesh. She was a part of him, and she should have occupied the first position in his heart. It was emotional neglect because, unknown to Uriah, Bathsheba having been violated by David, needed her husband's emotional support. It was physical neglect because of the fact that his close proximity to his home would have made it easy for him to have returned to her, if only for a short while.

There is always a danger when women are neglected.

Neglect is an avalanche waiting to happen and Uriah never saw it coming. This neglect led to a separation which, ironically enough led to his death when David sent him to the front line, instructing the captain of the army to make sure he was killed. The kingdom was humbled when Nathan the prophet confronted David about his adultery with Bathsheba, and the child adulterously conceived by David and Bathsheba died. This avalanche of neglect resulted in Uriah never seeing his wife again.

Men must treasure their wives by putting them in the forefront of their view. The must keep their wives in their spiritual and emotional sight. Not to do so is a subtle form of neglect which will inevitably damage the marriage. Men who neglect women have no understanding of the long term affect this form of abuse has on them. And since this relationship should be the first priority for every man, it is necessary that every man must reevaluate his value system.

How two people can become one is still a mystery today, but there is no mystery to how a man should treat his wife. He should cleave to her, thus demonstrating unwavering loyalty, making her his first priority, treasuring her above all others, pledging his undying faith. He must also take the time to listen, for in this, he will discovery the roadmap to her heart. No more mysteries. No more excuses. No more neglect. "For where your treasure is, there your heart will be also" (Matthew 6:21).

## Chapter 6

# When a Man Loves his Wife

*And this provides a good picture of how each husband is to treat his wife, loving himself in loving her,*
*(Ephesians 5:33 MSG)*

## WE ALWAYS HAVE CHOICES

*This is what the Lord says: 'Choose for yourself.*
*(1 Chronicles 21:11)*

**MEN** desire what they see. When a wife is no longer in her husband's view, trouble is not far away. When neglect, a form of spiritual and emotional abandonment occurs, it is no wonder that she will be lonely. And loneliness is the worse state a married woman can be in. A single person can find someone else to replace the absent lover, but a married woman, particularly one who married for companionship, can only wish and wait for her husband to come home.

I believe this is why Bathsheba was on the roof, (2 Samuel 11:2). In those days, the roof was the natural palace to be when you were waiting for someone to return, allowing as it did an opportunity to see them coming from afar. You could then make advance preparations for their return. But because of Uriah refusal to go home, Bathsheba never saw her husband again.

Some may think I am being too hard on Uriah. They may feel that he did not have a choice, because he was a soldier in David's army, but in this case, Uriah was not a soldier following orders. He was ordered by the king to go home, but he refused to go. Although King David was sending him under false pretence because David had secretly slept with his wife, Uriah did not know it. He chose not to obey the King's order because he felt it would be disloyal to his troops. Although he was next door to his own home, he chose his troops over his wife. That was his choice, and it would not be the only bad one he would make.

Consider some of Uriah's other choices. He was not afraid to stand up to the king and made a stand about not going home and eating and drinking with his wife (2 Samuel 11:11), but he made no stand about eating and drinking with the king and his servants. He had a problem with enjoying the company of his wife while his men were at war, but he had no problem with getting drunk. (2 Samuel 11:13). Uriah made choices that benefited him alone. He should have also considered his family. "If anyone does not provide for his relatives, and especially for his immediate family, he has denied the faith and is worse than an unbeliever" (I Timothy 5:8).

## HARD CHOICES

Our priorities help us to make the hard choices. A personal story will demonstrate this. I was faced with a difficult situation while serving in the Marines. A hurricane hit Guam while my family and I were on way back to Japan after a vacation. All available military fights from Hawaii to Japan were rerouted to Guam. This left me and my family stranded in Hawaii. The few flights that came available over the next couple of days only had one or two seats available, and I needed six. I had a choice to make. I could have left my family in Hawaii and reported back to Japan for duty within the allotted time. But if I had gone ahead without my family traveling with me, their seating priority would have been downgraded. It would have taken weeks before they would have gotten on a flight back home.

This choice was unacceptable to me, and so I stayed. This was a very hard choice for me to make because I was out of vacation days, and the consequence for not returning back to the base on time could have resulted in severe punishment. Despite this, I chose to stay with my family. The story did not end there. After a couple of days of being absent without leave, my commanding officer called and ordered me to return to Japan with or without my family!

I knew the consequence of disobeying a direct order, but my family was my first priority so I refused to leave Hawaii without them. I remained with them the nine days it took for us all to get on a flight together. Having my family as my number one priority helped me to make this difficult choice. When I returned, I was punished in a way that my commanding office thought best, but I knew in my heart that I had made the right choice. I chose my family over my own well being.

All choices have consequences. Men are faced with this problem of balancing their families and their career or similar types of choices every day. Having one's priorities in order, help make the right choice in difficult times, and it is well to know that God is there to guide us. Family is very important to God. Only two chapters in Genesis deal with creation, but the story of Abraham and his family takes up fifty. God expects men to take actions that will protect their families in difficult situation.

## COMMITMENT

*Husbands, go all out in your love for your wives, exactly as Christ did for the church—a love marked by giving, not getting. Christ's love makes the church whole. His words evoke her beauty. Everything he does and says is designed to bring the best out of her, dressing her in dazzling white silk, radiant with holiness. And that is how husbands ought to love their wives. They're really doing themselves a favor—since they're already "one" in marriage. (Ephesians 5:25-28 MSG)*

"When this happens, seven women will grab the same man, and each of them will say, "I'll buy my own food and clothes! Just marry me and take away my disgrace" (Isaiah 4:1 CEV). The book Isaiah talks of a day when seven women will look for one man to give them his name. They will be willing to marry the same man and share him with six others. This will never work because marriage is a union between two people that results in something greater than itself. It requires, an exclusive, committed relationship that result in them becoming spiritually one.

One man cannot have an exclusive relationship with

seven women. Furthermore, if he tries to do so, all seven relationships will suffer. Marriage is about commitment. The exclusive, solid relationship a husband has with his wife serves as physical, emotional, and spiritual support. When men fail at any level of relationships, all the other levels suffer along with it. Even relationships that simply involve friendship require commitment.

The original relationship was between Adam and Eve. It is easier for a woman to be in a committed relationship with a man because, when Eve was created, Adam was her companion. Unlike Eve, when Adam was created, he was alone. And it is possible, even today, for men to be alone and not lonely, particularly since, for some, it is easier than dealing with commitment. This may, in turn, lead them to avoid relationships, particularly that of marriage. But before making this choice, he should paint the picture he has in his mind and heart concerning relationships. The clearer the man paints the picture, the healthier the relationship.

"And this provides a good picture of how each husband is to treat his wife, loving himself in loving her, and how each wife is to honor her husband" (Ephesians 5:33 MSG). There are no words more powerful than that of a husband. A real husband will praise his wife because of the love he has for her in his heart. She can trust him because she is safe with him. She knows that his words are not motivated by an attempt to take advantage of her, either sexually or emotionally. She is already with him.

Marriage requires commitment. Not all men are ready to be husbands. When it comes to relationship as it pertains to marriage, some men get "cold feet." They view matrimony as "lock down" or the "old ball and chain." This approach is a negative view of marriage, portraying, as it does, the highest level of commitment as a loss of freedom. This view of relationships may cause men to shy away from dating and any sort of friendship that could lead to commitment, resulting in their seeking to distance themselves from the women in their lives. This "space" or lack of commitment can, over time, lead to neglect.

*Webster's Dictionary* defines space as the distance from other people or things that a person needs in order to remain comfortable. It also defines it as an opportunity for privacy or time to oneself. Space can be productive or counterproductive depending on how you use it. Space is not void of activity. Men like fishing, hunting, sports, and activities that give them time to themselves. And since they enjoy this space, they often assume that, because they enjoy it, it must be good for the relationship. As a result, they may head to the woods to be by themselves for extended period of time. And by "woods," I mean any place they can be alone, even a place in their minds.

However, no man is truly alone in these physical, emotional or spiritual woods since he must take his thoughts and desires with him. And there is always the danger of becoming lost there, like a Hansel who has no "breadcrumbs," in the form of a spiritual or moral guide, to lead him back.

## BONE OF MY BONE

*In this same way, husbands ought to love their wives as their own bodies. He who loves his wife loves himself. (Ephesians 5:28)*

Adam declared that Eve to was the bone of his bone and flesh of his flesh. When a man loves his wife, he loves himself. He loves her as though she's a part of his own body. "After all, no one ever hated his own body, but he feeds and cares for it, just as Christ does the church" (Ephesians 5:29). When Uriah neglected Bathsheba, he neglected himself. She was a queen all along, but he did not realize it. Men today, like Uriah, are living with queens, but they are too busy to notice it. Some have even left their homes and wives unprotected, just as Uriah did when he chose to sleep on the porch with the servants rather then go home and attend to his wife. She was so much a part of him that when he neglected her, he neglected himself. This is a basic and fundamental principle that all men must learn. "He who loves his wife loves himself" (Ephesians 5:28).

Just as Christ loved the church and gave himself up for her, husband should love their wives. When a man gives himself to his wife, she becomes more then she would have been without him. They are no longer two, but one. "For this reason a man will leave his father and mother and be united to his wife, and the two will become one flesh" (Genesis 2:24). When a man loves his wife, he loves himself, and together they are able to share this love with the world. This makes for better relationships, neighborhoods, and communities. When this union takes place, we are all better because of it.

# CHAPTER 7

# Ounce of Prevention

*An ounce of prevention is worth a pound of cure.*
*Henry de Bracton's De Legibus (c. 1240)*

## OUNCE OF PREVENTION

THIS proverb, which has been around for hundreds of years, is still true today. Prevention involves advance knowledge. It means doing things now that will have positive future impact. That is why we get polo or flu shots. Prevention can be more powerful than a cure because it has the potential to make the cure unnecessary. The little things we do up front can have monumental impact down the road.

Have you ever given your number to someone you just met? He seemed like a nice guy. You thought your could trust him. After all, it was just your phone number. What harm could come of that? If you had only known at that time that he would later become a pest or ever worse, a stalker, you would never have done this. You received the information that you needed after you took action. This made the information less valuable.

I have talked to many women who say, "Had I known

this about him up front, I would never have wasted my time with him in the first place." The "this" varied from woman to woman, but the "had I known" was the common thread that ran through all their accounts. These women told me how these men, some thieves, others scam artists, alcoholics, child molesters, drug dealers or adulterers, took advantage of their bodies, money, resources, emotions, and most importantly their hearts.

How differently things would have turned out if these women had some foreknowledge. "But understand this: If the owner of the house had known at what hour the thief was coming, he would not have let his house be broken into" (Luke 12:39). The earlier the information is known, the greater the impact. The question then is not when did the thief break in, but rather when did the owner find out. Had the owner known the hour, he would have taken the steps needed to keep the thief from stealing his goods.

Although this is one of the shortest chapters in this book, it is probable one of the most valuable. An ounce of prevention is still worth a pound of cure. The insight you put into practice today will have a profound impact on your life tomorrow. It involves putting the power of prevention to use by knowing the ounce of information before you take the pound of action. This small change can save you from a lot of heartache and wasted time. What we don't know can hurt us.

## MAXIMIZING YOUR BRAIN POWER

Information helps to keep people from taking advantage of us, and it is important to realize that it can come from multiple sources. What we see, hear, smell, taste, and touch sends millions of signals to our brain. Some of this information such as smelling smoke, or hearing a fire alarm is more valuable than others, including the noise of traffic and yesterday's sales prices. Each bit of information we receive from our senses is labeled, categorized, cataloged, and stored in our brains. We all need to maximize the power of our brains to sort though the tons of information we receive every day.

Because we spend a lot of time processing information, we can harness the power of our brains by relating information we have already stored away to the new information we are receiving. And since our brain categorizes information, it can instantly make connections which are timely and useful. Memory experts use this categorizing and cataloging technique to teach others how to recall large amounts of data in a short period of time.

Relating men to that from which they were formed follows the same premise, making it easier to separate the good from the bad. Just as there is toxic soil, so there are toxic men. If you are able to identify the latter, you can save yourself a good deal of heartache.

## HEED THE WARNING SIGNS

In nature, there are instances in which the soil has become so contaminated that entire areas are quarantined. No one is allowed into the area except for those who have special training in dealing with that type of problem. These experts go in cautiously, wearing special uniforms and using special equipment. If someone without special equipment and training tried to deal with that sort of contamination, they would probably do serious harm to themselves. To keep this from happening, roads are blocked, signs are posted, and alarms are triggered to warn anyone approaching of the impending danger.

Like dirt, the men who fall into the toxic category have similar characteristics in that they are a danger to the spiritual, emotional, and physical well being of others. Pay attention to the signals and use your God-given built-in alarm system. When danger approaches, there are signs and signals that trigger warnings of impending danger. These brain signals are more valuable than any posted signs and more powerful than any roadblocks.

Heed the warning signs. Preventing trouble also means avoiding trouble. Since some men are as dangerous as quicksand, mudslides, and sand traps, once identified, they should be avoided at all costs.

Stay clear of toxic men! Don't try to understand them or make sense out of why they are the way they are; just stay clear of them. Leave the analysis to the experts. This chapter will help you to acknowledge the wealth of information that your brain has already stored. The alarm has been sounded, and the flag has been raised!

## QUICKSAND

Avoid quicksand. As defined by *Webster's Dictionary*, it is something that readily yields to pressure, or something that entraps you. Quicksand lacks stability and is incapable of supporting anyone or anything. It is as fluid as liquid, and it has the potential of drowning anyone that comes in contact with it. Men who are quicksand will take you down with them because they will suffocate you with their problems. Their previous relationships, legal, credit, and financial problems will become so overwhelming that you regrettably get swallowed up with them.

Quicksand has a couple of very distinct qualities that will help you identify it. First, it is void of life. Nothing can take root in quicksand. Similarly, men like this have nothing stable about them. Their job, home, car, family, and friends are all in a constant state of flux. They never establish roots, and because they are fluid, they will never be with anyone or anything long.

Secondly, quicksand is subsurface. Quicksand pulls everything down to its level. Everything about these men is less than what it should be, and if you form a relationship with them, you will inevitably be less than you could be, as well. Because they have no resources of their own, you will constantly be asked to support their substandard life style. Once your resources are depleted, these men will move on to the next victim.

But quicksand, in any form can be avoided. You just need to ask a few simple questions such as, "Do you have a job?" "How long have you worked there?" "Where do you live and how long have you lived there?" If his answers hint of instability, run! Do not try to get to know him or think that you can change him. No job, no conversation! No stable home life, no relationship! This may sound harsh, but he must first be responsible for himself. Quicksand is very dangerous ground, and you may get drowned if you get too close to it. To prevent this from happening, listen to your inner alarms and keep on moving!

## MUDSLIDES

Along with quicksand, you must also avoid mudslides. Mud is a mixture of slimy, sticky material usually mixed with water. Mud can also be abusive or malicious remarks as in the phrase "slinging mud." Mudslides are created when mud makes its slow moving descent, covering everything in its path, pulling everything it comes in contact with down with it.

Similarly, men who are mudslides are slick and slimy, and they always get carried away taking others down with them. They can never establish a long term relationship because everything around them is usually messy and muddy. These men often have unresolved relationships, child support, and legal issues. Instead of cleaning up their act, they move from relationship to relationship leaving their mud behind for others to deal with. These men muddy the water with one bad relationship after another. They should be avoided because, when they slide on to the next relationship, they will not only leave behind a mess for you to deal with, but they will also take pieces of you with them.

Here is a tip on how to avoid such a mudslide. These men are bundles of unresolved issues. First, determine the extent of these, and then pay attention to the warning flags which, if the man is married, may involve some form of separation. Perhaps he is not supporting his children. Ask yourself how can a man that is not taking care of his own responsibility help you with yours? Or perhaps the majority of his possessions are in someone else's name which means that the other person will always be connected with him at some level.

Don't let mudslides slip up on you. Mudslides are too messy to hide. Evaluate the answers to your questions. You don't need to take on someone else's downward spiral. Give mudslide men time to clean up their act before they muddy your life with theirs.

## SAND-TRAPS

Avoid sand-traps. Sand-traps are different than mudslides or quicksand because mudslides and quicksand are dangerous. A sand-trap is a more of a hazard in that all it requires of you is to be aware of its presence so that you can go around it. A sand-trap stops the forward momentum of whatever comes in contact with it. It is usually man made, and it resides in close proximity to your goal.

Some men are like the sand-traps that you see on golf courses. Ask yourself, why is there sand in the mist of all this green grass? This is not the place where sand is supposed to be. These men often become part of the entourage of highly successful men, riding on their coat-tails and using them to pick up women. At best they are pests, and at their worst emotionally draining. Fortunately, they are easy to identify because these men live their lives through others. Their conversations begins with the "my" as in, "my boy, "my partner", "my friend." Because they live their lives through their friends, they always have to check with them before they make a move. Their life follows the schedule of others and their resources are in the wallets of others. They will also be all-too-eager to catch the high flying ball of a successful woman.

## TOXIC SOIL

Finally, avoid toxic soil which contaminates whatever comes in contact with it and can cause death. There are always labels to warn you. Take care to read them. They range from "drug dealer," to "convicted felon," to "pimp," to "pedophile," and may well include, "wife abuser."

Heed the warnings. Some women are meeting men on prison web-sites, a warning sign if there ever was one. Others are knowingly becoming involved with pimps and players. Toxic men kill whatever they come in contact with, a slow, harsh death, laced with malice. Toxic men will kill your dreams, joy and ambition, and put your family, and friends at risk. Ignoring the warning signs can have dangerous consequences.

I listed toxic men last because, already having been labeled, they are the easiest to avoid. Read the warning signs and go the other way! It is just that simple. If you were to see a sign posted that read "DANGER, MINE FIELD AHEAD!" would you keep going to see if it was true? If another sign read, "STOP! BRIDGE OUT!" would you keep driving anyway?

Killer, Pimp, Thug, toxic men often wear these labels like badges of honor. They believe these titles give them creditability in the streets. The fact that they know what they are and are proud of it is part of the danger. They are revolving doors of past mistakes and future regrets.

Real men refuse to let their past define them. There is no "x" in front of their names. Real men, despite their past, are now judges, doctors, lawyers, engineers, pastors, police officers, and firemen. These men have redefined their past failure by their current success. This gives them creditability in all walks of life.

# POUND OF CURE

Doing the little things up front prevent heartaches down the road. An ounce of prevention is worth a pound of cure. Prevention involves advance knowledge. Prevention has the potential to make the cure unnecessary. Making good use of your experiences will enable you to be able, in an instant, to avoid toxic men. I have already categorized these men as quicksand, mudslides, sand traps, and toxic soil. Because the next four types are not as easy to identify, I will spend the next four chapters addressing the subject of men who could be classified as hard, stony, thorny, and fertile ground. The ground represents the heart of men. If you study the ground, you will study the heart.

## CHAPTER 8

# The Wayside: The Hard Heart

*I will remove from you your heart of stone and give you a heart of flesh.*

*(Ezekiel 36:26)*

## HEART OF STONE

"THOSE by the wayside are they that hear; then cometh the devil, and taketh away the word out of their hearts, lest they should believe and be saved" (Luke 8:12 KJV). Bob grew up with a hard heart, in good part because his father abandoned his family while he was still a little boy, and his mother, forced to work two jobs, was gone most of the time. Born and raised in the inner city, Bob had seen and experienced more than most adults by the time he was twelve, as well as having learned to live without the affections or approval of others. It was only natural that he developed a thick skin to protect himself. Little by little, Bob's heart was hardening until he slowly developed a heart of stone.

As an adult, hard-hearted Bob had little or no sympathy for others. Determined not to be hurt again, he developed an

"I don't care" attitude, referring to himself as hard but fair. He made it a point to never say "I am sorry" or "I love you," and deemed hug and kisses as unnecessary displays of affections. Bob's heart of flesh because a heart of stone. This heart of stone is considered the wayside.

Throughout this chapter, I will use the term "wayside" because it is synonymous with the term the Bible uses in the book of Mark chapter four. "And it came to pass, as he sowed, some fell by the wayside, and the fowls of the air came and devoured it up" (Mark 4:4 KJV). The wayside, which means, literally, "off the path," is land adjacent to a road or path. More of a "where" than a "what", and as such represents, metaphorically, the place where seeds can be sown, seeds which give birth to life, and in the context of which I speak, the hearts of men.

When young men are excluded from love, nurturing, caring, concern, and correction, they are essentially cast to the wayside where poor soil inevitably makes their hearts hard and bitter. And since this hardness of the heart is invisible to the human eye, some women unknowingly connect themselves with these men who were never properly cultivated during their formative years. Oftentimes these women mistakenly plant their seeds of love, respect, and resources into wayside men. And when they do, they usually get little or nothing in return.

Many women are currently in relationships with wayside men. While looking for their knight in shinning armor, they encounter and fell in love with "hard-hearted" Bob," a man who knows nothing of intimacy.

## BEWARE OF WAYSIDE MEN

Any woman that is married to a "hard-hearted" Bob is in a one-sided relationship, one that dashes all hopes of closeness and mutual respect. When the woman gives and the man does not, she is left to be her own source of emotional support. This happens as a result of not having the right information up front. It is also the result of misinformation. On the surface, it may not be clear that the wayside man is an enigma void of emotions.

Beware of wayside men because they do not come with warning labels. Unlike the men previously discussed, these, although approachable, appear to be dark and mysterious. Their air of mystery makes you want to go below the surface. A little digging won't hurt, right? Wrong! Whatever you dig up will never be enough. You will be reduced to becoming an archeologist of the emotionally dead.

Look to the heart. Ask questions that will reveal the heart of a man, questions like "Have you ever been in love?" or "When was that last time you told someone "I love you?" Find out the extent of his emotional reserve. Explore how he feels about some of the things that are important to you. Make sure that he is capable of sharing his heart.

Although wayside men cannot be eliminated, they can be avoided. Understanding the basic characteristics of a wayside man can help you to avoid planting your resources into ground that is barren. The wayside cannot be cultivated because it is the wrong location. The seeds must be move to more fertile ground before they can become plants.

# CHARACTERISTICS OF A WAYSIDE MAN

Wayside men have distinguishing traits, first and foremost of which is their inability to express compassion. Hard and unfeeling, they have hearts of stone. Because of this, they are often cold and insensitive. They see crying as weakness and believe tears have no place in the life of a real man. Having come up the hard way, they have learned to do without. "Easy come, easy go" or "You win some, you loose some" are phrases which characterize their outlook on life. But as everyone who knows how to relate to others realizes, nothing comes easy. Everything has a cost. Relationships come with a high emotional price tag and someone has to pay it. Unfortunately, in these instances, the woman usually ends up paying, while the wayside men end up playing.

Wayside men cannot handle internal pressure and all relationships come with a certain amount of this built in. And although these men often seem hard enough to handle any sort of stress, this is far from the truth. The hardness within them will only allow pressure to build up until, having reached maximum capacity, they will either explode or leave.

Wayside men also avoid responsibility because it brings too much stress with it, stress they would prefer to relegate to others. I know of a man who will only stay with a woman as long as she does not make any demands on him. If she ever dares to ask him to help carry the load, he finds the nearest door and runs to the next woman who will allow him to live with her, free of demands. If you are in a relationship with a wayside man, you will always be the one taking responsibility. If you take them in, they will consider themselves doing you a favor just by being there. Their presence is their only contribution to the relationship.

Guard your heart because wayside men return nothing. You will sow and not reap, and you will give and not receive. You may plant love, but you reap nothing. You plant peace, but you reap nothing. You will give, but you will never receive in return. Any woman dealing with a wayside man is in danger of risking and losing everything she has to give.

You have probably encountered a wayside man. He was the one that did not understand why you helped others, making efforts which, to him, constituted a waste of time and resources. His philosophy is that other people get what they deserve. The wayside man would also seek to stifle your emotions. He is not move by your tears, viewing them as an attempt to control him. He would rather confront you than comfort you, and make war rather than peace.

Wayside men can be very deceiving. To the eye, they seem to have the qualities that women are looking for: strength, firmness, durability, and straightforwardness. This perception could not be further from the truth. Their hardness is often mistaken for strength. These are similar qualities, but they are not the same. Hard men are also difficult, unfeeling, unyielding. Wayside men cannot be instructed. They will not yield to anything. They are not truly strong.

Void of emotions, as they are, the best they can do is to become angry. This "when in doubt, anger out" attitude will be the only emotional tune they will every play. Wayside men also refuse to assume responsibility. Having made it this far in life without giving an account of themselves, they do not intend to start now. They will continue to think this way until God replaces their hearts of stone with a hearts of flesh.

## A NEW HEART

*Now there arose up a new king over Egypt, which knew not Joseph. Therefore they did set over them taskmasters to afflict them with their burdens. And they built for Pharaoh treasure cities, Pithom and Raamses.*
*(Exodus 1:8, 11 KJV)*

Pharaoh was a wayside man. He did not know God, nor did he seek after the things of God. His desire was to please himself. All the building and statutes in Egypt were a tribute to him, not to his creator. All his decrees were given to exalt himself. There was no authority outside of his. Wise in the ways of the world, he was ignorant to the things of God. Pharaoh did not have the courage or the desire to do what was right. He was hard, stubborn and difficult, an authority unto himself. Like Pharaoh, wayside men are their own authority.

In order for a wayside man to change he must submit to a higher authority. God dealt with Pharaoh. But although he suffered the death of his oldest son, he still refused to come under God's authority. He, along with Egypt, endured one plague after another, yet Pharaoh remained and an authority to himself. Thanks to his inability to acknowledge the power of God, he put all of Egypt at risk.

Wayside men are difficult to change. They have become comfortable and settled on the wayside, outcast for so long that they now welcome being left out. This act of defiance becomes their badge of honor, an integral part of who they are. The heart of the wayside man must be brought to God because only God's word can penetrate it. "Is not my word like as a fire? saith the LORD; and like a hammer that breaketh the rock in pieces?" (Jeremiah 23:29 KJV).

Words alone cannot transform a wayside man. "And these are they by the way side, where the word is sown; but when they have heard, Satan cometh immediately, and taketh away the word that was sown in their hearts" (Mark 4:15 KJV). The word that was sown never sunk in. It was merely on the surface, waiting for Satan to come and snatch it out. Only God can transform a wayside man. "A new heart also will I give you, and a new spirit will I put within you" (Ezekiel 36:26).

## LOCATE THE HEART

*For where your treasure is, there your heart will be also.*
*(Matthew 6:21)*

"Location is everything!" This term has often been repeated in business conversations. Something as simple as the side of the street a business is located on can determine its traffic pattern. This subtle different could be the distinguishing factor between the success and failure. Some years ago, when I lived in Albany, Georgia, I bought my first home. It was located in the heart of the city, only minutes away from the downtown, the mall, and other major attractions. I selected this particular house because the trees on this road were in a straight line and their branches came together to form and arc at the top. It was spring, and the flowers were in full bloom. When the sun hit the trees, the flowers seem to come alive and dance in the sunlight. This beautiful archway led the way to the end of the road where my house was located. The fact that this house was located at the peak of the incline on this road meant very little to me at the time, but in less then a month, it would mean everything.

I closed on the house in June of that year, and one month later, tragedy struck. A flood came through and devastated the city. Several lives were lost and thousands of homes were destroyed. My house was spared, for one reason alone, because of its location. You see, location is a byproduct of destination. Everything at the bottom of the incline was flooded; everything at the top was not.

Just so, a wayside man's heart has found itself where it is because it has been located in a place where others have trampled over it, where the enemy has been able to come and steal the good that was stored in it. It does not matter how much you fertilize the earth by the wayside, for it will only be trampled on again. But just as soil can be moved elsewhere, to a place which will allow it to become fertile, so men's hearts can be relocated to a place where it can hear the word of the Lord.

The man that refuses to heed to God's word has, spiritually speaking, built his house on the spiritual wayside. "But everyone who hears these words of mine and does not put them into practice is like a foolish man who built his house on sand. The rain came down, the streams rose, and the winds blew and beat against that house, and it fell with a great crash" (Matthew 7:26-27).

## THERE IS HELP FOR "BOB"

There are many "Bob" in world today. But he should not despair, nor should those who love him. Every man has the opportunity to put spiritual principles into practice, and in doing so get a new perspective on life, one full of hope and promise. "Therefore everyone who hears these words of mine and puts them into practice is like a wise man who built his house on the rock. The rain came down, the streams rose, and the winds blew and beat against that house; yet it did not fall, because it had its foundation on the rock" (Matthew 7:24, 25).

Wayside man's heart must be transformed. Being outside the will of God has dangerous consequences. This man will be controlled and driven by the elements. He will be subject to the changing winds that drive the course of this world. His entire life will be controlled by the foundation on which it has been built. His house will fall, and it will be a great fall unless he can be persuaded to give himself over to God. He may be your son, husband, brother, or father, but you must take him to the Lord in prayer. If at all possible, get him in the place where he can hear the word of God. It will transform his heart.

The wise man's heart is in the right location. He is not wise because of his past experience, but rather because he has chosen to put the word of God into practice. His foundation is now a rock, and his authority is the word of God. The elements cannot move him because he is founded upon a rock. No longer is he governed by his own authority. No man is an authority unto himself. His very breath, as well as the essence of his spirit comes from God. "Man shall not live by bread alone, but by every word that proceedeth out of the mouth of God" (Matthew 4:4 KJV). God's word can relocate the hard heart of a wayside man to a spiritual oasis of love, peace, joy, and emotional prosperity. Then and only then will the wayside man be able to return back more than what was planted in his heart.

# CHAPTER 9

# Stony Ground: The Unstable Heart

*He is a double-minded man, unstable in all he does.*
*(James 1:8)*

## BEWARE OF STONY GROUND

"SOME fell on stony ground, where it did not have much earth; and immediately it sprang up because it had no depth of earth" (Mark 4:5 NKJV). It was the news of the neighborhood. Right across the street, the police had surrounded the house of my seemingly quiet neighbor, who, having shot his wife, barricaded himself inside. When the first police officer arrived on the scene, my neighbor shot him as well. For hours the police attempted to negotiate with this obviously unstable man. This stand-off finally ended in my neighbor's back yard when a plain clothes police officer jumped him as he tried to escape.

We later found out that this tragedy was a result of his wife becoming so fed up with his emotional instability that she finally got up the courage to leave him. Prior to that incident, the only thing we knew about him was that he was the man with the big St. Bernard dog. As it turned out, our quiet neighbor was not so quiet after all. Everyone was shocked to find out that such a violent man had been living in our midst. We all found out the hard way that unstable ground is dangerous ground.

Stony ground is unstable ground, even though a smooth surface may make it appear to be otherwise. Men who are stony ground have serious emotional issues, some of which may be attributed to what has happened to them in their past. Because this emotional imbalance has found its way to their heart, it can be set off by the slightest thing. Men who are stony ground go from hot to cold, from extreme happiness to depression. Some of these men were victims of abuse themselves. Some have even suffered sexual abuse at the hands of other men. Whatever their story, they often battle the urge to become abusers themselves. This inner struggle causes a tear in the masculine soul which creates, in turn, an internal imbalance that fosters emotional instability.

Beware of stony ground for it breeds violence. According to the FBI, an average of 1400 women a year are murdered by their husbands or boyfriends. Conservative estimates indicate two to four million women of all races and classes are battered each year.

Stony ground is dangerous ground because, when a man does not have control over his emotions, he does not have control over his actions, even if it means that he may harm or kill himself. A man that is capable of taking his own life is capable of taking someone else's life as well. Men who talk of suicide often kill the object of their affection. Many women live on this dangerous ground.

## SURFACE SUCCESS

Stony ground is different from wayside ground. Wayside ground is in the wrong location, while stony ground is in the wrong condition. When a man's heart is stony, it will not allow anything to take root in it for long. Stony ground, even when covered with a layer of fertile soil, produces that which it cannot sustain. Seeds planted here will put down roots in vain. With its roots wrapped around a stone, the plant eventually loses its connection to the soil, its source of life. The plant becomes an island unto itself.

Like the stony ground, a stony man is one who has become disconnected from his roots. He has no desire to know the very people who gave him life. Because he has disowned his own family, he will feel the need to establish a new one. Because of this, a stony man will often propose marriage very early in the relationship. He will talk of love and display strong affection. He will also become possessive, because his new family is his life and the only roots he has.

On the surface, a stony man may appear attractive, perhaps even desirable. He may communicate well and have accumulated all the material things a woman desires, such as cars, money, and houses. But he will lack the real things needed to sustain life because these things come from within. A man's connection to his family and his heritage helps to keep him grounded. When a man loses contact with his origin, he loses contact with himself.

Stony ground is very deceptive ground. On the surface it looks and feels like the real thing. The stem from the seed broke through the earth. A vine appeared. A new life has been created. All of these things are major milestones. The sun is now shining on the new plant, and it is on the upward climb to the sky. This is the beginning of success. But it is only surface success, because, although whatever is planted into stony ground rises to the top quickly, the roots beneath the rocky surface cannot sustain it.

King Saul was an example of stony ground. Not only was he tall, strong, and handsome, he was a monarch. In no time at all he went from being from the least of men, to the first king of Israel. But he lacked confidence. When it was time to accept his position as king, Saul hid himself among the food and clothing supplies (1 Samuel 10:21-22) because he was afraid of rejection. This fear made him a shallow and insecure man, someone who needed the constant approval of his people, without which he did not consider himself a success. He measured himself by the approval of others which is, in itself, rocky ground.

Everything about Saul was on the surface. Saul was selected solely because he was a lot taller than everyone else and not because of his character and conduct. "They ran and brought him out, and as he stood among the people he was a head taller than any of the others" (1 Samuel 10:23). Furthermore, he was selected by the people and not by God. "But you have now rejected your God, who saves you out of all your calamities and distresses. And you have said, 'No, set a king over us'" (1 Samuel 10:19). Saul was king, but he was not a good choice for a mate for several reasons. He had an evil spirit. He had insecurities. He had an anger problem.

King Saul was insecure and emotionally unstable even before he was king. After he became king, Saul went from loving David to hating him all in the same breath. When a man loses control of his emotions, you cannot predict what he will do from on moment to the next. Like Saul, men who are stony ground are often insecure, emotionally unstable men. You are not the cause of this sort of man's insecurity. It was there before he met you, and if he does not get help from God, it will be there when you are gone.

## LOVE AND HATE

*Whoever does not love does not know God, because God is love.*

*(1 John 4:8)*

If a man does not love, protect, and preserve his wife, he is operating outside of God's word. God requires more than lip service. A man may set his own standards and think that, if he lives up to them, nothing will ever be his fault. He will blame the woman in his life for his abusive behavior, and will never accept full responsibility for his actions. But abuse never comes from God. God's standards demand more of a man than his own standards ever could. The word of God provides man with boundaries and limitations which prevent him from ever abusing anyone, even himself.

When a man keeps God's word, he is living up to His standards. "Others, like seed sown on rocky places, hear the word and at once receive it with joy. But since they have no root, they last only a short time. When trouble or persecution comes because of the word, they quickly fall away" (Mark 4:16, 17). Man must have the word of God in his heart. "I have hidden your word in my heart that I might not sin against you" (Psalms 119:11). The word of God must be allowed to soak into the heart of man in order to nourish his spirit. Only then can a man be kept from sin.

"Man cannot live by bread alone" (Matthew 4:4). God's words turn the stony heart into one filled with a love which protects, and perseveres. This love is not easily angered. It must be described by words that are meant to protect, and not by words shrouded in mystery that gain power from the hidden message they contain. Such as, "There is a thin line between love and hate," or "love hurts."

These sorts of statements are harmful because they associate love with hate and hurt while, in reality, there is more than a thin line between love and hate. Hate hurts. Hate starts with pushing and shoving and escalates to punching and slapping which may lead to choking, kicking, and killing. Hate results inevitably in rage.

Love is the opposite of hate. Love brings about life. Love heals. Love is patient and kind. "Above all, love each other deeply, because love covers over a multitude of sins" (1 Peter 4:8). Love is a powerful force that endures all things without fail. Generated, as love is, from the good that is in a person's heart, it is predicated on knowledge of God. Because of God's word, you can live and abide in love, a place of peace and harmony. Those who love are of God. "And so we know and rely on the love God has for us. God is love. "Whoever lives in love lives in God, and God in him" (1 John 4:16).

The Bible is clear; those who love are of God and those who hate are not. Love and hate are as far apart as the east is from the west. A person traveling from east to west would circle the entire earth, and still be traveling east. Like east and west, love and hate are at the opposite end of the spectrum from each other. No man can claim that he loves a woman who has become the object of his abuse, particularly since he has been commanded by God to love his wife as he loves himself. "In this same way, husbands ought to love their wives as their own bodies. He who loves his wife loves himself" (Ephesians 5:28).

## SELF LOVE

Men who are stony ground can be verbally and physically abusive, using words to control others. Words are powerful, and they have consequences. When a person finds themselves in an abusive relationship, their first response is usually to rationalize the situation, to try to make sense out of it. Often they will try to find words or sayings that justify staying in the relationship. They do this out of love for the other person, but they must love themselves first. The relationship is secondary to their emotional and physical well being. The most important conquest is the one that sets us free. "No, in all these things we are more than conquerors through him who loved us" (Romans 8: 37).

Self-love is one of the most powerful forms of love. No one can really control another person's action, but they can control their own. There may be times when the love of self compels a woman to leave the man she loves. (Providing a man the space necessary to get the help he needs is the highest form of self-love.) Every person has in them the power to separate themselves from harmful situations. This could one day save that person's life.

Stony men must be dealt with or their mental and physical abuse will escalate. The first step, however, is for the woman to recognize that she is not equipped to carry his emotional baggage and that, as his internal struggle reaches a critical mass, she may be in danger of being harmed physically. If you or anyone you know is currently being physically or emotionally abused, seek help now! Confide in family and friends. Allow them to help get the professional assistance needed. No one helps themselves or the relationship by allowing abusive behavior to continue.

No man has the right to abuse another person either physically or emotionally. Any man that does is responsible for the consequences of his own actions. You still reap what you sow. Abuse, often stemming from the abuser's internal instability, is not the fault of its victim. He cannot abuse the person he claims to love, and then use his love for her as his defense.

Walking around on egg shells will not stop the abuse. Stony men can snap in an instance because they need professional help. Their emotional instability makes it impossible for them to be in a secure, healthy relationship. Skilled professionals will have to till the rocky soil, and this will not be easy, particularly since stony man will not be receptive to your seeking help. He will want to resist. Self-love will compel you to take action.

Stony ground is the dangerous unstable ground of the man that has lost his connection to God, someone who has deliberately tied himself to those who have enough resources and patience to constantly feed his ego. He will gamble with your money and your heart. He will say and do almost anything to maintain his facade. Worse, you will not be allowed to share in his success. His insecurity will keep you at bay because his happiness is tied to the approval of others.

Self-preservation is one of the strongest human desires. You may not be able to change the soil, but you can stop planting in it. In the few years it took me to write this book, over 6,000 women have been killed by someone who claimed to love them and millions more have been abused. The men who committed these crimes were not motivated by love. Love is patient; love is kind. It is not envious, boastful or proud. It is not rude, self-seeking, or easily angered. Love keeps no record of instances of being wronged. Love does not delight in evil but rejoices with the truth. It always protects, always trusts, always hopes, always perseveres. Love never fails (1 Corinthians 13:4-8).

## Chapter 10

# Thorny Ground: The Deceitful Heart

*The heart is deceitful above all things and beyond cure. Who can understand it? (Jeremiah 17:9)*

## THORNY GROUND

*Still others, like seed sown among thorns, hear the word; but the worries of this life, the deceitfulness of wealth and the desires for other things come in and choke the word, making it unfruitful. (Mark 4:18-19)*

IN this chapter we will discuss the fact that thorny ground is the most deceitful of the four types of ground, primarily because of its deceptive appearance. Like the serpent that deceived Eve in the Garden of Eden with the false hope of a promising future, men who are thorny ground use images and half-truths to get what they want. With thorny ground, you only see the prize and never the pricks, the flower and never the thorns. Thorny ground is more than just a type of soil. It is a spiritual condition that exists in the heart of men.

Satan was the original example of thorny ground. He

desired to be more powerful than God, and this caused him to lose his place in heaven (Isaiah 14:14-15). Not only did he deceive himself with blind ambition, but he was responsible for Adam and Eve's fall, as well. First, he deceived Eve by telling her that she would never die if she ate of the fruit of the tree of the knowledge of good and evil. "You will not surely die, the serpent said to the woman. For God knows that when you eat of it your eyes will be opened, and you will be like God" (Genesis 3:4-5). Then he made his words even more enticing by telling Eve that she would be as wise as God if she ate the fruit. Not only did Eve bite, but she convinced Adam to do so, too.

When Adam followed Eve's example, they both became aware of good and evil, and in so doing, lost their innocence and damaged their relationship with God. They were both expelled from the Garden of Eden for having disobeyed God's word. "But you must not eat from the tree of the knowledge of good and evil, for when you eat of it you will surely die" (Genesis 2:17).

Eve's desires to be as wise as God, kept her from seeing the truth behind Satan's words. She failed to see that he never had her best interest in mind, and that his real objective was to separate her from God. "Then the LORD God said to the woman, "What is this you have done?" The woman said, "The serpent deceived me, and I ate" (Genesis 3:13). Satan's words ensnared Eve, and her life and Adam's were changed forever.

## SNARED BY WORDS

*Then you are trapped by your own words, (Proverbs 6:2 CEV)*

Like Satan, men who consist of thorny ground will use words to entangle others. At first, they will pretend to care about the person, but once their victim is in their trap, they will turn on them. When I think of thorny ground, the image of a pimp often comes to mind. I remember the first time I ever saw such a man. It was in the early 70's. He drove a big flashy car and wore a flamboyant hat and platform shoes. His jewelry was loud and overbearing. You could see him coming from a mile away. He was a walking billboard that screamed "STAY AWAY." My first thought was to wonder how anyone could allow themselves to associate with him.

Then he began to speak, smoothly, poetically, soothingly. He had an answer for every question, and a saying for all occasions. He spoke of turning poverty into prosperity and hurt into hope. He appealed to the disenfranchised, downtrodden, and lonely.

The purpose of this man's words was to keep his victim listening and lingering. He needed to make women his allies. Allegiance was a part of his plan. He wanted to make his words hers so that she could play a part in ensnaring herself. But this allegiance was only temporary on his part. Once she was trapped, his attitude changed. He became controlling, threatening, and harsh. The words once used to draw her in were now used to put her down and keep her there.

And so we see that the danger thorny men present is that they know how to use words to produce a false sense of hope and trust, both based on false promises. Thorny ground will produce something tangible, bright and beautiful, but the beauty and the thorns go hand-and-hand. You cannot have roses without thorns. Beware of thorny ground. The thorns are not there to keep you from the prize. On the contrary, they are there to entangle.

## CHARACTERISTICS OF THORNY GROUND

One of the key characteristics of thorny ground is that it looks good from a distance. I remember picking tomatoes as a little boy. Unknown to me, some of the tomatoes had become disconnected from the vine. From a distance, they all looked just as good as the others, but once I picked one up, I quickly realized that it was rotten underneath. To make matters worse, the stench of it stayed with me long after the tomato was gone. It took me a while to separate the good tomatoes from those that were rotten, but eventually I learned.

Thorny men are the same way. They look good from a distance. They spring up like a healthy tomato, but they are rotten underneath. Jesus said in John 15:4 CEV, "Stay joined to me, and I will stay joined to you. Just as a branch cannot produce fruit unless it stays joined to the vine, you cannot produce fruit unless you stay joined to me." Thorny men have lost their connection to God and their fruit will rot. The word of God has been choked from their hearts by the deceitfulness of wealth and the desire for other things.

Be careful. Thorny ground is very productive because it springs up quickly. In that lies the problem, because it takes time to build character. Overnight success and long term success is not the same thing. How did this man reach his success? Some men will do almost anything to become successful. They will cheat, steal, or lie their way to the top. Because these men have the trappings of success today does not mean they will have them in the future. “Don't bother your head with braggarts or wish you could succeed like the wicked. In no time they'll shrivel like grass clippings and wilt like cut flowers in the sun” (Psalms 37 1-2 MSG). Thorny men are so preoccupied by the accumulation of riches that they don’t even realize that the rot has set in.

Don’t be deceived by what you see. At first glance, thorny men’s lives may seem glamorous. But as time goes on, the truth will surface. The house of cards will crumble. Nothing they have will be able to stand the test of time because they never took the time to build on the solid foundation supported by a core set of principles and values that are put into practice everyday. “But everyone who hears these words of mine and does not put them into practice is like a foolish man who built his house on sand” (Matthew 7:26).

Thorny men base their hopes and dreams on money. They will tell you about the wonderful life that you can have with them, but their words are the only prize you will ever get. Remember that the devil took Jesus to a mountain and showed him all the kingdoms of the world and their splendor below. “All this I will give you," he said, "if you will bow down and worship me” (Matthew 4:8-9). Satan offered Jesus the world even though it was not his to give. This was an attempt to get Jesus to worship him instead of God. Satan made an offer that he could not fulfill. He hid behind his words.

Like Satan, these thorny men will try to keep you distracted with their words. They will talk more about what they can do for you and very little about who they really are.

They will not allow you to know as much about them as they know about you. Thorny ground is surrounded by secrecy. For example, there will be excuses why you cannot interact with their family. This is part of the power of the thorns. If you knew the truth about them, you would not get pricked.

## THE POWER OF DECEPTION

Some years ago, I knew a woman who became involved with the wrong man. Out of the blue, he showed up on her doorstep, and told her that he could not get her out of his mind, and that he was falling in love with her. He went on to say that he knew he could trust her and he wanted her to do something for him. He gave her a briefcase full of money and told her to count it for him and return it back to him on the next day. He did not want to answer any questions concerning where the money came from, but he assured her it was on the up and up. He also added that he had not already counted the bills and that he would take her word for the amount. She never saw the deception coming. She was so impressed with him because he told her that he loved her, and he entrusted her with a great deal of money to prove it.

Because she was confused as to what to do, she came to me, and I, not being under his spell, knew exactly what was going on. First, I told her that she was being set up. This man knew exactly how much money was in the briefcase. He was testing her to see if he could trust her with future transactions. Next, I told her to give the money back, uncounted, and to leave him alone. This man had trouble written all over him, and if she was not careful, she would get caught in something that she would not be able to get out of. Although she thanked me for the advice, she left without telling me what she had decided to do.

Months went by. I did not see her again until the day before she was to move out of town with her new found friend. She had given him all the money back, and had continued to see him. Since I had last seen her, not only had he been generous, but he often entrusted her with his money, and later with packages which she never opened. Whenever she asked about their contents, he explained away as "business papers."

Finally all of this came to an end when this man showed up at her doorstep. He confessed that he had used her to hold and deliver drugs. Fearing that the police were onto him, he planned to leave town and take her with him. He could not, he explained, afford to have her out of his sight until things cooled down. She told me that, when she refused to go, he threatened to kill her. Trapped and afraid for her life, she realized now that she was entangled in a situation which she could no longer handle.

Still, she said that she had decided to leave town with him. She was afraid to go to the police for fear of being arrested for her involvement, leaving her with no choice except to go with him until things cooled down. She was sad to say that although she had been with this man for all these months, she knew nothing about him. Now she was worried because she had no idea where they were going, and she feared no one would ever see her again. I never did.

My friend never intended things to go as far as they did. She, like many others, believed she could walk away from any situation if it ever got out of control. Such was not the case. She had been too caught up with the prize to notice the thorns. Many may say that they could see that danger coming from a mile away, but you still have to get close to see the thorns. And the closer you get, the more likely you are to become entangled with the wrong man. The best advice for you is found in 1 Thessalonians 5:22 KJV, "Abstain from all appearance of evil."

## PACKAGES OF INFORMATION

My friend missed all of the warning signs that this man was giving her all along the way. First, she had no idea of where he lived or what he did for a living. This was a warning sign that something might be wrong. Secondly, although he came to her house, she was never allowed to go to his. This was a big red flag! Thirdly, his entire life was shrouded in secrecy. He hand delivered her sealed packages on a regular basis. She was never allowed to see what was inside of any of those packages. This was a big "danger" sign. Finally, she never met any of his family of friends, and she barely knew anything about him. The signs were all around her, but she was too caught up in superficial details to notice.

This situation should serve as a warning to us all. Like my friend, we all get packages of information delivered to us daily. The thorny man's life, whether public or private, provides you information about his past if you will only allow yourself to see it. His past cannot be totally hidden. Vigilance and watchfulness will help you to see the thorns. The most important thing to remember is that you must heed the warning signs once you see them. There are always warning signs, some more obvious than others. All provide valuable information that might one day save your life.

## WARNING SIGNS

Although warning signs are all around us, not all are easily recognized. Here are four indicators of thorny ground to look for. The first begins in the mind of the woman. Beware of the "that's my husband" syndrome. This sign is for the women who have a tendency to lay emotional claim on a man that they know little or nothing about, but believe that by laying first dibs on him, they will be able to keep other women at bay. The danger is that this approach plays right into the hands of thorny men who want nothing more than to create an illusion of commitment because inwardly they know that they are not husband material.

This illusion is dangerous because this fantasy causes many women to rationalize away any information that does not contribute to keeping the illusion alive. Without the fantasy, nothing about him is real. His positive qualities exist only in their minds. These women have fallen in love with their own fantasy of someone who they hope will love them in return. But in reality, everything about this man must be "assumed." He will of a certain never be able to demonstrate true love. One thing is certain. This thorny man is not husband material.

The second warning sign is the lie or half-truth. Thorny men must never be taken at their word unless you want to risk discovering, late in the relationship, that he is married or living with another woman. Be careful. Your heart is the one at stake. Perform your own background check. Google him if you must, but be vigilant just the same. Don't rely on his words alone. Recognize that he is practiced in deceit. If things seem strange or odd, it is most likely your woman's intuition at work.

Warning sign number three of thorny ground involves the condition of his spiritual relationship which means more than whether he goes to church or not. Men who are thorny ground hear the word of God, but the word never makes it to their heart. "Still others, like seed sown among thorns, hear the word; but the worries of this life, the deceitfulness of wealth and the desires for other things come in and choke the word, making it unfruitful" (Mark 4:18-19). This spiritual unfruitful condition may be a subtle warning sign, but a powerful one just the same.

His spiritual life can be measured by an examination of his character and conduct, as well as his morals and values. What are the bases of his value system? Where do his morals come from? Is he at peace with God? Is he at peace with himself? Men, who are torn internally, cover it up externally. They use flashy clothes to cover spiritual failure, and flashy cars to cover up a corrupted heart. Their desire for material wealth becomes their substitute for the word of God. They will talk a good game while losing the spiritual battle. These men will have to use other people and an accumulation of things to compensate for their lack of spiritual depth. This requires more than the ability to quote scriptures or to say I am sorry. This requires morals and values that are consistent with a higher standard.

The fourth and final warning sign is the man's attempt to persuade you to sell yourself short. You have a lot to offer. Some men will seek to prey on your weakness, so use your woman's intuition. You may be single, but not lonely. If he is married, walk away! No exceptions! If he has kids, find out the extent of his relationship with them. If he is not helping to support his biological children, he will not support you. If he lives with a woman or is in a relationship with one, walk away! You deserve a whole man not a piece of one. The type of man you attract will be directly related to the type of woman you believe yourself to be. If you believe you are the best and deserve the best, then you will attract the best men. These men will come your way if you do not yield to attempts by lesser men to persuade you to sell yourself short.

## MONEY WITHOUT A MISSION

*The words I have spoken to you are spirit and they are life. (John 6:63)*

"The heart is deceitful above all things" (Jeremiah 17:9). Thorny ground is deceitful ground inhabited by pimps, players and wannabes, among others. These men are fertile, but although they have money, they have no mission; they are flashy, but they have no substance. Covered as they are by the illusion of success, they will ultimately consume all of your resources. To keep this from happening, maintain a strong connection with your family and friends. They are not blinded by him. But remember that because they are a source of reliable information, he may seek to keep your from them.

God's word should be your primary source of advice. It will illuminate your situations and shine light on the thorny men. The best and most effective information will come from God's word and from those that have love for you in their heart, love that has stood the test of time.

You cannot see thorns from a mile away, but you can heed the warning signs that indicate danger up ahead. Listen to friends and members of your family that you can trust. They have an objective view of the situation that is based on a realistic view of how this man really is. The open, honest advice from friends and family should never to be taken lightly. This advice provides the insight to the other side of a man's character. His lack of a solid spiritual foundation will always be one of the biggest and most telling "warning" sign. This sign should never be ignored.

Thorny men are deserts in the misdt of a spiritual oasis. These men are like the wind. Their whole life is based on an illusion that is not a true reflection of what is in their hearts. Their flowery words are meant to distract you from their thorns. The cares of this world and the deceitfulness of riches deafen them to the word of God. Heed the warning signs and stay clear of thorny ground!

## Chapter 11

# Good Ground: The Noble Heart

*But the seed on good soil stands for those with a noble and good heart,*

*(Luke 8:15)*

## GOOD GROUND BEARS GOOD FRUIT

*Thus, by their fruit you will recognize them (Matthew 7:20)*

"THE steps of a good man are ordered by the Lord" (Psalm 37:23 KJV). Good men do exist, but you have to look patiently to find them, surrounded as they are by wayside, stony, and thorny men. You can tell if a man is good or not by determining whose authority he is under. Stony, thorny, and wayside men are their own authority, but the steps of a good man are ordered by the Lord. How do you know if you are dealing with good ground? You will know it by the fruit it bears. Good ground bears good fruit.

Before you enter into a relationship with a man, be aware that what he has produced thus far is a reflection of how he has lived his life. Matthew 7:18 says "A good tree cannot bear bad fruit and a bad tree cannot bear good fruit." What is fruit? Fruit is the product of actions over time. It is the return on a man's investment of time and energy. "Still other seed fell on good soil. It came up and yielded a crop, a hundred times more than was sown" (Luke 8:8). Look at a man's past as well as the present. A man cannot blame his current actions on his childhood. He is a man now, and must take responsibility for what he does.

To really understand a man, you must act, and look not only at the present, but what has shaped him as he developed into manhood. "And the LORD God formed the man of the dust of the ground" (Genesis 2:7 NKJV). God made man from one of the most powerful substance on earth, soil. "But the seed in the good soil, these are the ones who have heard the word in an honest and good heart," (Luke 8:15 NASB).

The Bible is full of examples of noble men with a good heart. These men return more than what was planted into them in their past. They gave more than they received, and they added to the lives for all those with whom they interacted. Good men are those who understand that God has a plan for their lives, and seek to fulfill it.

The way a man relates to others is often a reflection of the way he interacts with God. Noble men have noble hearts. Men like Abel, who was killed by a jealous brother because he offered a better sacrifice to God (Gen. 4:8), and those who are like Enoch, a God fearing man who walked so closely with God that he did not see death (Gen. 5:21-26). There is Noah who obeyed God with out question and built and ark, saving the world from extinction (Gen. 6:14-22).

Other good men like Moses, who although he was raised in Pharaoh's house, chose to suffer with the people of God, and as a consequence, became one of the greatest leaders in biblical history. And then there was Abraham, a man who was so faithful that he was willing to offer up his only son to God as a sacrifice. Good men like Isaac, Abraham's son, and Jacob his grandson received the covenant and inherited the promise of God. In addition, there were great leaders like Joshua, who led the people of God into the promise land against great odds. Men like Caleb fought faithfully by Joshua's side. All of them sacrificed themselves for the good of others. Others, like Samuel the prophet, dedicated their lives to the service of God. Men of valor like David and Samson defeated great opponents to free the people of God.

Just as they did in biblical days, good men exist today. They are all around you, although since what is inside them distinguishes them, they are not always easily apparent. But only put them to the test as you would the fertility of ground, and you will soon see precisely who they are. As for the testing process, good men won't mind.

## REFLECTIONS OF THE HEART

*For the Lamb at the center of the throne will be their shepherd;*

*(Revelation 7:17)*

The center of a field is where you can find the most fertile soil. It is also where the ground is most stable. Likewise, the person that is centered has distanced himself as far as possible from disaster. He understands that personal victories come before public victories, and that being honest with one's self comes before being honest with others. He retains the word of God, and values all that God has created. "But the seed on good soil stands for those with a noble heart, who hear the word, retain it, and by persevering produce a crop (Luke 8:15).

Man's heart is at the center of his being, and his life will be a reflection of what is stored in it. It is where his values come from. How important is honesty to him? What is his relationship with God and others? Does he align himself to the word of God? Everything must be in its proper place. Someone who is successful in business, but a failure in his personal life is not centered. "What will it be for a man if he gains the whole world, yet forfeits his soul?" (Matthew 16:26). A good man's values come from within. He does not measure himself by the yardstick of his material possessions, but rather by the virtues stored in his heart. "The good man brings good things out of the good stored up in his heart," (Luke 6:45).

Being centered also means being balanced. His private life must measure up to the public life; he must be able to provide for himself before he can provide for others. He cannot depend on others to prop up his reputation. He must stand on his own.

Just as fertile ground is productive so must a good man be the same. His actions must demonstrate that he creates for the good of all, and not simply for himself. Just as fertile ground converts simple seeds into an abundant harvest, good men know that what is in their heart will be fruitful. They know as they give from their heart that it will be returned to them in overflowing abundance. "Give, and it will be given to you. A good measure, pressed down, shaken together and running over, will be poured into your lap. For with the measure you use, it will be measured to you" (Luke 6:38).

Fertile ground will return more than what was planted. When you sow your seeds in this kind of ground, you will receive a yield greater than what you have given, just as good men serves as a catalyst to your dreams and desires. They multiply whatever is planted in them and their seed never runs out because the greatest returns come from the heart. Yielding is the fundamental principle by which God operates. You cannot give God an apple seed and get an apple seed in return. If you give God an apple seed, God will give you a tree full of apples that, in their turn, are full of seeds.

And so it is that one should never measure a man by his possessions. True riches are to be found in his relationships rather than his material wealth. "A man's life does not consist in the abundance of his possessions" (Luke 12:15). A man is greater than his possessions. A good man will have people in his life who love and respect him. His relationship with people will always supersede his relationship with things. These relationships reflect what is stored in his heart.

## SENSITIVE TO THE REAL YOU

A good man is sensitive to the real you. He knows your passions and embraces them. He knows your dreams and encourages them. He understands your boundaries and respects them. He is sensitive to you. He laughs when you laugh, sings when you sing, and cries when you cry. He is aware of the things that take place below the surface. He is really and truly in tune to the spirit of who you are.

I know first hand that it is possible for a man to connect with the heart of a woman. I married right after I graduated high school, and I set out to be in tune with my new wife. Young as I was, I thought this meant noticing a change in hair-style or weight. I worked hard to make sure I paid attention to physical changes, no matter how subtle. But later I discovered that this was just the tip of the iceberg. I later became so in tune with her that, even when we were thousands of miles apart, if she wanted me to call, I would know it. I knew her thoughts without her ever having to tell me. When we were together, it was as though I could read her mind. When something bothered her, it bothered me, and what was in her heart was real to me.

But, although I had acquired this sensitivity, I did not value it. As time went on, a great deal was changing right before my eyes, but I was too busy to notice. I spent so much time working on my own personal growth that I forgot about her. I no longer felt her pain. I didn't notice her loneliness. Because I was riding on past successes, I was oblivious what was going on right before my eyes. As the years past by, I became so busy and self-absorbed that I lost the sensitivity which had enriched our original relationship. And ultimately I lost the relationship, as well.

In nature, once you plant a seed, it goes through various stages of change. When the seed is below surface, it needs covering, and when it is above ground it needs support. Fertile soil makes the necessary adjustments to make the seed productive. The seed is in the heart of the ground. This covering is what keeps the seed protected from the elements. Good ground is sensitive to the changes in the seed. It is able to sense and feel what is happening above and below the surface.

The seed must remain in the heart of the soil where it can be protected. There, the seed is safe and secure. Good men carry those they love in their heart, protecting and providing for them. "If anyone does not provide for his relatives, and especially for his immediate family, he has denied the faith and is worse than an unbeliever" (I Timothy 5:8).

There are subtle changes that take place in women, some at the very core of her being. This is no problem for the good man because he is a part of her. He is like the soil that supports and nourishes her. Fertile soil must detect the changes in that which it embraces, and be strong enough to support the plant. Good men must do the same.

Good men are stable, able to change when change is necessary, able to protect you when you are most vulnerable. They will not let you fall or take advantage of you. They will cover you when you are down, and they will support you when you are up.

Time is the true test of stability. That is why it is not wise to rush into relationships. At the beginning, everything may seem wonderful, but it is necessary to trace certain patterns in his life, patterns that will allow you to make predictions about the future. If the man you love has a faithful past, he will most likely have a faithful future. Patterns must be studied upfront. The longer a woman is in the relationship, the less she can depend on her judgment. Once emotions are involved, she is no longer able to make an unbiased decision. When you understand the pattern of a man's life, it is easier to make decisions about the future of your relationship. Because you are at the center of his heart, a good man will be sensitive to the real you.

## CONTINUOUS PURSUIT

There was a rich man in the Bible who desired to be in God's kingdom. From the time he was a child, he kept all of God's commandments. And as a man, he came to Jesus seeking to know what he needed to do to inherit eternal life. Jesus told to him to sell all he had and give the money to the poor. The young man, surprised by Jesus response, sadly turned and walked away unwilling to submit to the Jesus' request. Because he was very rich, he had too much to easily let it go. The young man believed in his heart that he had done more than enough to inherit eternal life.

But he ignored the fact that the best soil soaks up all the rain which makes it rich. The man that seeks after what his spirit lacks becomes rich in spirit. The man that does not desire the things he needs spiritually may be materially rich but he is destined to remain spiritually poor. Although there is no such thing as a "perfect" man, good men strive for perfection. Good men work every day to be better. Knowing that they are capable of sin, these men submit themselves daily to the authority of God. It is through him that they lack nothing.

Every man must choose daily to be the best he can be. I personally know men who know they need anger management, but refuse to get it. I know of men who do not have a high school diploma, but refuse to go after it. Some men wear their pride, titles, riches and fame like a badge that entitles them not to go after more. They believe that what they have makes up for what they lack.

The rich man cited above had money, but he lacked compassion. Jesus told him that his unwillingness to care for those less fortunate, that in fact, his riches were a part of the problem because he trusted in them more than God. He was being controlled by his wealth, and he didn't even know it.

Jesus knew the man's material accumulations controlled him rather than the other way around. Had he been in control, he could have let his wealth go, but it controlled him. It does not matter whether it is, money, drugs, alcohol, anger, or pride, if a man cannot control it, he will be at its mercy.

No man can be good without God. Because he will always be at the mercy of whatever has taken the place of God. When a man submits himself and all that he has to the authority of God, he demonstrates that he is in control of his life and all its accoutrements. In the case of the man who could not follow Christ's command, he lacked the ability to let go of what was keep him from getting closer to God. Jesus was not interested in the man's riches, but rather in his soul. A good man will always be in continuous pursuit of that he does not have.

## QUEST FOR GOD

*There is none good but one, that is, God.*
*(Mark 10:18KJV)*

A woman looking for a good man must go beyond what she sees on the exterior. "Do not consider his appearance or his height, for I have rejected him. The LORD does not look at the things man looks at. Man looks at the outward appearance, but the LORD looks at the heart" (1 Samuel 16:7). The heart is the key. A noble heart desires God. This man desires whatever he is lacking despite the good he already has. Just as a poor man desires riches, foolish man wisdom, and a hungry man food, so should a proud man desire humility. If a man does not desire what he does not have, he will always be lacking.

The desire for God should always be paramount. "But seek first His kingdom and His righteousness, and all these things will be given to you as well" (Matthew 6:33). God is the source of all that is good. If a woman expects to find a good man who has ignored God's word, she will be disappointed. He may be rich, famous, well-educated, and handsome, but he will always be at the mercy of whatever he has in the place of God. Good men seek God daily. It is the quest for God that makes a man good. He has God in his heart. This keeps him centered, balanced, and stable which, in turn, makes a good man noble.

# Chapter 12

# Immature Male

*And Jesus grew in wisdom and stature, and in favor with God and men.*

*(Luke 2:52)*

## FROM IMMATURITY TO MATURITY

*When I became a man, I put childish ways behind me.*

*(1 Corinthians 13:11)*

PHYSICAL GROWTH is almost non-optional. If a man eats the right food, he will grow. Emotional growth is a lot more complicated, particularly since his emotional development is connected to that of his spirit. Any man whose spirit, the core of his being, from which his emotions, passions, desires, fidelity, and faithfulness are generated, is stunted will not be developed emotionally. This spiritual development gives man the solid foundations that he needs to grow into his full potential. The depth of his inner being produces the depth of his character. His emotions, key elements in the conflict we have been discussing will be generated out of this invisible spiritual reservoir.

The fact that wars of the emotions can only be waged by two adults is complicated by the fact that some men keep their childish ways well into adulthood. If the man fails to put his childish ways behind him, he will choose to play games rather than engage in a meaningful dialogue. In this case, the woman will be forced to assume the role of parent which is a frustrating position into which to be put since there is no satisfaction in parenting an adult. At best, these women may be able to get their immature males to behave most of the time.

Immature males are boys in men's clothing. They look like men on the outside, but inwardly they cling to their boyish ways, still playing games, and in need of someone to take care of them. Webster defines a boy as a male child from birth to adulthood or an immature male. Boys become men not when they reach a certain age but when they move from immaturity to maturity which implies a certain degree of physical, spiritual, and emotional development.

Lastly, some males grow up physically, but never mature spiritually or emotionally which makes it easy for women, at first glance, to be deceived into thinking that they are dealing with men. This deception can be very frustrating to women who expect the outer male to reflect the inner man. As a result of the frustration of dealing with immature males, some women have become leery of all men, tending to see "all" men as boys needing to grow up. This chapter will help you to separate the males from men. Below are several characteristics of an immature male.

## GROWN MALES

Though it requires effort, it is possible to separate the men from the boys. Real men welcome this distinction, while immature males will rebel against it. Let take a look at four key distinctions. First, grown males lack internal development. They look like men on the outside, but inwardly, they are still boys. The have height, but not depth, money without mission, and biceps without precepts. All of their attractive features are external while, inwardly, they are filled with instability. In the Old Testament, Saul was selected as the first king of Israel because, outwardly, he was head and shoulders taller that all the other men. But he lacked the heart of a king as well as the character development needed for leadership. Like Saul, many males are incapable of accepting responsibility.

Responsibility is one of the keys to manhood. Men accept responsibility for their actions, but grown males do not. With them, it is always someone else's fault. They see themselves as always right and everyone else as wrong. Saul blamed the people for not obeying God (1 Samuel 15:20). He did not see himself as being responsible for his own choices. Someone else is always to blame, even, at times, God. In this "not my fault" make-believe-land, immature males do no wrong, and no one can convince them otherwise.

Secondly, grown males, such as King Saul, are underdeveloped emotionally. Saul was insanely upset because the people cheered more loudly for David than they did for him (1 Samuel 18:7, 8). Because of this, he threw a childish tantrum, during which he tried to kill David. Like Saul, grown males cannot accept someone else's success, nor will they accept constructive criticism. Emotional time-bombs, these men display childish behavior that often can rival that of a two-year-old. Like little boys, if they don't get their way, they take their marbles and go home. You will know you are dealing with an immature male when he displays childish behavior.

Grown males are also underdeveloped when it comes to dealing with finances. This is more that just simply not having money in the bank. Lacking a sense of financial responsibility, they view bills as snares instead of obligations. Because they feel trapped by long term responsibility, they are often dependent on someone else to take care of money for household expenses. If you marry one of these men, you will be the in-house banker.

Thirdly, grown males are sexually immature, tending to measure themselves by what is between their legs, the place where their manhood is located. These men consider their sexual encounters as a badge into a club called "MEN." They measure themselves by the number of their female conquest or "notches in their belt." This, along with their irresponsibility and lack of internal depth, inevitably results in multiple infidelities. Boys will be boys. These are the men who will try to excuse their infidelities on some secret male code that tells them that the degree to which they can claim masculinity depends on the number of sexual partners they can accumulate. This is far from the truth. If a grown male's manhood is between his legs, rest assured that there is nothing of substance in his heart.

Next, grown males lack confidence, with the result that they must hide behind their baggage. King Saul lacked self-confidence. Although he was head and shoulders taller than everyone else, he was found hiding behind the food and clothing supplies (1 Samuel 10:20-22). In an attempt to avoid being detected for what they are, some men use externals, including what they are wearing and the cars that they drive to hide internal deficiencies. This will never suffice. Confidence, a function of maturity, comes from within and needs no such disguises.

Finally, these men live outside of the word of God which requires character and commitment to the truth in the face of pressure. The weight of God's word crushes those who view it as an unreasonable expectation. As long as they continue to live outside God's word, they can continue to measure themselves by the standards of a boy in a fairy-tale land, free from responsibilities. These men are children in men's clothing seeking to avoid God's word which can only be borne by real men.

There are grown males among us have not been through the fire, and as a consequence, they are like unrefined steel, waiting to become the finish product. These untested, unfinished, irresponsible models will not perform as advertised and should be returned to their manufacturer, God, as soon as possible.

## REAL MEN HAVE UNLIMITED POTENTIAL

*Then God said, "Let us make man in our image, in our likeness,*

*(Genesis 1:26)*

A real man, physically, emotionally, and spiritually developed, is a part of God's plan. God makes males into men. He takes them into his hand and forms them in his image. The word of God is the key to man's spiritual development. "Man does not live on bread alone, but on every word that comes from the mouth of God" (Matthew 4:4).

All males have the potential to become real men, and the word of God is the catalyst for this transformation. The Bible is not a book to be read in church only. It is the owner's manual which provides the reader with the operating instructions needed to help man perform at his optimum potential. Man requires maintenance that can only be performed by the manufacture or creator. He is subject to recall by his creator because, at any given time, his model may require a spiritual upgrade. This spiritual upgrade is what will keep him running on all cylinders. This spiritual upgrade is what transforms males into men.

"The LORD God took a handful of soil and made a man. God breathed life into the man" (Genesis 2:7 CEV). Because a real man has God's spirit, he will be forever learning, and becoming increasingly capable. Nothing in nature will ever surpass him in knowledge or potential. Man is not God, but he has been created in God's image. God created him to have dominion over the whole earth and all therein, therefore, he was made to be the wisest of all God's creations. All other creatures were destined to be subject to him.

God gave man a mind unlike any other, making him able to reason, debate, recall, and create, as well as to will. Man's brain is the greatest of all brains. He only needs ten percent of it to function, but God gave him the other ninety percent so he would have unlimited potential. What you see is only a fraction of all that man is capable of becoming.

## REAL MEN HAVE BOUNDARIES

Real men need God's word and spirit to be complete. Jesus said, "The words I have spoken to you are spirit and they are life" (John 6:63). God formed man from the dust of the earth, giving him contour and structure. "In the beginning was the Word, and the Word was with God, and the Word was God" (John 1:1). The Bible refers to the "man without the Spirit, someone who, does not accept the things that come from the Spirit of God, for they are foolishness to him, and he cannot understand them, because they are spiritually discerned" (1 Corinthians 2:14). When man becomes one with the word of God, he becomes one with God. This oneness gives man boundaries and limitations. Man is a free moral agent, but he is not free to sin against God.

"And the LORD God formed man of the dust of the ground, and breathed into his nostrils the breath of life; and man became a living soul" (Genesis 2:7 KJV). Man's breath belongs to God. His life is in God's hands and not his own. "So our bodies return to the earth, and the life-giving breath returns to God" (Ecclesiastics 12:7 CEV). The breath that is in man is one with the word of God. "And Jesus answered him, saying, It is written that man shall not live by bread alone, but by every word of God" (Luke 4:4 KJV). Man needs God's word to live. He can never live up to his full potential without it.

Immature males have the potential to become real men, but they have to make a conscious decision to grow up. This is more than lip service. This involves real change. It is possible for them to put their childish ways behind them. "When I was a child, I talked like a child, I thought like a child, I reasoned like a child. When I became a man, I put childish ways behind me." (1 Corinthians 13:11). Temper tantrums and childish tirades must cease. Man's very thought process must change. "Brothers, stop thinking like children. In regard to evil, be infants, but in your thinking be adults" (1 Corinthians 14:20).

Every male is required to make the transition to manhood which has nothing to do with age but everything to do with the development of his spirit as it conforms to God's word. This process will bring about emotional development that is equal or greater than a male's physical development and reveals more about his manhood than his height alone could ever demonstrate. His words will be powerful, his steps will be sure, and his conduct will be honorable. This is male development at its finest. Immature males move into their manhood when their heart conforms to the word of God.

## Chapter 13

# "A Woman's new Affirmation"

*Then God said, "Let Us make man in Our image, according to Our likeness. (Genesis 1:26 NKJV)*

## NEW AFFIRMATION

*Beware of Dogs (Philippians 3:2 KJV)*

"ALL men are dogs!" Have you ever heard or said this. It seems to be common for some women who have been hurt and taken advantage of by men to say things like this. Although this statement may apply to some men, it does not apply to all. Men are like soil which can be tilled, watered, and fertilized. Don't allow your focus to be solely on men who, for one reason or another, do not measure up. There are plenty of "beware of dogs" warning signs all around. Although these signs give us insight on what to avoid, they provide very little directions. To really get somewhere, you need directions.

Your words help to guide you to your intended destination.

What you say influences what actions you take. Like the highway signs that are repeated along every road, positive insight must be constantly reinforced. Unlike our eyes which allow us to see what is ahead of us, real insight demands that we tap into spiritual insight, which will, in a sense, allow us to see around corners. This insight begins with the words we say, and they end with the actions we take. Let us, for the purpose of analogy, replace "warning sign" with "affirmation."

What is an affirmation? *Webster Dictionary* defines it as a positive assertion. It is a single or series of positive statements that reflect the attitude and sentiment of those making it, as well as a moral compass for all that submit to it. These guidelines can serve as an affirmation of faith. By repeating them, you give them power. They should include the purpose, potential, and declaration God has already made for man. Let this new affirmation about men reflect your new study of the earth and the men who come from it. Your insight about man should be based on what God has already said about him.

First, your affirmation should include the purpose for God creating man which was that he wanted him to have dominion over everything (Genesis 1:26). God gave man the right to rule the earth and all things on it. Real men are leaders who have their spiritual, emotional, and physical lives in check. Woman's positive affirmation reinforces this fact.

Secondly, in making man in his image, God gave him the gift of unlimited potential. The earth gave birth to everything that we can see, and everything we use, from cars and computers, to oil and nuclear energy. Just so, no matter what man has accomplished, he like the earth from which God made him, is capable of doing more.

Finally, our affirmation should be consistent with what

God has already said about man. Anyone who aligns themselves with the word of God will be successful. "This book of the law shall not depart out of thy mouth; but thou shalt meditate therein day and night, that thou mayest observe to do according to all that is written therein: for then thou shalt make thy way prosperous, and then thou shalt have good success" (Joshua 1:8 KJV). An affirmation that reflects God's word will also cause *you* to prosper. For I know the plans I have for you," declares the LORD, "plans to prosper you and not to harm you, plans to give you hope and a future" (Jeremiah 29:11).

God has a plan to make man's future a prosperous one. As a result, you should be careful not let your words limit him. "You might get trapped by what you say; you might get caught by your own words" (Proverbs 6:2, NCV). Check what comes out of your mouth against the word of God. Never allow your words to be the limiting factor. You create our own affirmation everyday. Let it speak of yours and the blessings and prosperity of others.

## THE "CANINE TEST"

*So Gideon took the men down to the water. There the LORD told him, "Separate those who lap the water with their tongues like a dog from those who kneel down to drink."*

*(Judges 7:5)*

There is no doubt that separating the men from dogs will not be an easy task. That is why it is very important for women to heed the warning signs. "Beware of Dogs" signs are posted to warn others that danger is up ahead. Although the sign does not describe the particular breed of animal, it is clear that, whatever sort of dogs it is, it is one that poses danger to you. The sign is your last warning before you put yourself in harm's way. To ignore it could be disastrous. It is analogous to God's warning about certain types of men who like a wild pack of dogs, rip and tear others with their teeth.

Because God is opposed to men who behave like dogs, he gave Gideon the "canine test," instructing him to reject all men who, in lapping water like dogs, demonstrated that their only concern was their own physical need. In so doing, these men displayed qualities that were contrary to that of true men. Gideon did not try to reason or understand them, he simply sent them home. Like Gideon, don't waste yourself on men who are like dogs.

To begin with, doggish males repeat the same action over and over. They mark their territory. They go around in heat. The men with Gideon were exhibiting these dog-like characteristics. These men got down on their hands and knees and put their face into the water. They lapped water like a dog. They didn't consider the fact that they were on the battlefield. They were not watchful. Like a dog in heat, they were oblivious to their surrounding. They only considered themselves and their immediate fleshly desire.

Comparing some males to dogs is an insult to "man's best friend" everywhere. Dogs are loyal and protective. Calling men dogs is counterproductive because real men will feel needlessly insulted and those who deserved the insult will not respond to it. Furthermore, if you constantly say all men are dogs, over time, you will start to believe it. And once you believe it, you run the risk of treating <u>all</u> men like dogs.

To make a clear distinction, study real men. Like bank tellers who knows a counterfeit bill when they see one, you must also know real men well enough to immediately recognize an imposter. Use the Bible to tap into your spiritual vision because a man will always be more than what you see.

Spiritual words will provide you with spiritual insights. As you study God's word, you will be reassured that real men do exist. Don't worry about the others, particularly since there are so many breeds. Once you know the real man, you will be able to pick out a dog from a mile away. Follow Gideon's example and look for manly qualities in men. Meanwhile, send the dogs back home.

## BLESSED BY GOD

Good men do exist, but if women expect to plant God's words into men's hearts, they first must test the soil before putting their own heart, talent and resources, which are their precious seeds, at risk. Good seeds need good ground, and the ground is the heart of men. No ground can lay uncultivated and not grow up into a wilderness. If nothing is planted in heart of boys, if they are neglected, a wilderness will arise. Our streets are full of young men who grew up wild because no one planted order, self-respect or values in them. They will, of necessity, grow into men who have had nothing of value planted in their hearts, and they will give nothing of value in return.

There is still hope. Women have a special responsibility because God has entrusted them to be the caregivers of the world. This is why mothers are a very important part of God's plan. They are the first ones to plant seeds in the life of a young man, seeds that will be the first to sprout. Mothers sow and the whole world reaps. Women have the power and opportunity to shape the rest of a man's life with her words and actions. The hand that rocks the cradle still rules the world. A mother's words can shape the lives of all the future men in the world. These young men will grow up to be wonderful husbands and fathers.

Eve was the mother of us all so we should constantly be reminded of the trust God has placed in mothers. It is all the more important, therefore, that their words should be based on the word of God through which he has given them invaluable insight. This insight can be used to help man accomplish salvation. Women are a part of God's blessing plan for man. "He who finds a wife finds what is good and receives favor from the LORD" (Proverbs 18:22).

"And God blessed them, and God said unto them, be fruitful, and multiply, and replenish the earth, (Genesis 1:28 KJV). Good men and women working together have the power to create. If women plant seeds into a good man's love, the return will be a loving family. Her love will come back to her as sons, daughters, and grandchildren. It will come back as intimacy, affection, and admiration. A good man will return the love she gave with interest. He will be a reservoir of love that she can always draw from. Connect with the right man, and your well will never run dry and your resources will never run out. This is prosperity at its best.

A good man can help you to prosper. A man reaps what he sows. (Galatians 6:7). Good men have the potential to take what is planted in them, multiply and return it. To prosper means to grow and flourish. "Give, and it shall be given unto you; good measure, pressed down, and shaken together, and running over, shall men give into your bosom" (Luke 6:38 KJV).

The field is the world, the seed is the word of God, and the ground is the hearts of men. The process of sowing and reaping works both positively and negatively. It can bring for good or evil, diamonds or dynamite. Plant wisely or you may reap what someone else has planted. The world receives what you plant, and you receive what the world plants. "Thus the saying 'One sows and another reaps' is true" (John 4:37).

Good men do exist, but there is no magical formula for finding them. You will have to use your God-given intuition and the knowledge gained from these pages to separate them from the masses. You are the light of the world! Continue to be a light for yourself. All things begin and end with you. Men are dirt, woman's new affirmation!

## Chapter 14

# Is He Ready for You?

*For dust you are and to dust you will return.*
*(Genesis 3:19)*

## STEPS OF A MAN

*A man's steps are directed by the LORD. How then can anyone understand his own way? (Proverbs 20:24)*

**BECAUSE** you are the most important part of any relationship, this book ends in the same place it began, with you. You alone are responsible for so much. It is very doubtful that anyone would consider marrying a ten-year-old boy. He is not mature or responsible enough for a serious relationship. The person that married the ten-year-old would be headed for trouble. Age alone does not guarantee that a man is ready for a commitment. He must be evaluated from head-to-toe to ensure he is "relationship healthy." This is different from normal health since it involves man's spiritual, emotional, and physical well being.

Is he ready for you? To determine if a man is "ready," you must examine the steps that he has taken to lead him to manhood. Does he have order in his life? This is important because the creation was based on God's order. The heavens and the earth were created first, and man was created last. Just as the earth was created before man, order comes before relationship. God did not place man into the world until it was ready for him. Likewise, he did not place man in a relationship with woman until he was ready for her.

If a man is to prove that he is relationship ready, bonds must be developed in the right order and at the right time. For example, in order to determine whether or not a man respects his relationships, we must consider the fact that his respect for others is governed by respect for himself. He can never give more than what is in him to give. If he is not honest with himself, he will not be honest with others. If he is not faithful to himself, he will not be faithful to others. And if he quits on himself, he will quit on others. The development of lasting bonds will be a key indicator. Self-respect does not come with age; it comes with maturity.

You can tell if a man is ready for a committed relationship by the successful fruit he brings forth. "Make a tree good and its fruit will be good, or make a tree bad and its fruit will be bad, for a tree is recognized by its fruit" (Mathew 12:33). An immature man will be surrounded by the fruit of irresponsibility, and his relationships will be under-developed.

## BIG THINGS FIRST

*May your whole spirit, soul and body be kept blameless*
*at the coming of our Lord Jesus Christ.*
*(1 Thessalonians 5:23)*

To fully determine if a man is ready for a committed

relationship, you must evaluate the development of the total man, his spirit, soul, and body. Many books have been written addressing man's physical and emotional condition, but his spirit needs to be addressed as well. Without understanding the spiritual aspect of a man, he can never truly be understood, particularly since his spirit gives way to his emotions and his desires. Man's spirit gives life to his body (James 2:26). He is spiritual before he is emotional. His spirit shapes his inner man.

God created man so that his spirit would provide order and direction to his mind and body. Order is very important to God. Just as you cannot put the eggs in the cake after you take it out of the oven, so it is that no man can be at peace with himself or others until he has made peace with God. Relationships cannot be rushed. They take time to develop. A man must clearly demonstrate that he is ready for a committed relationship approached in the right way with first things first.

I would like to share a story I read in the International Sunday School lesson about a teacher who wanted to illustrate to her young students the importance of doing things in the right order. She started with two empty cylinders, as well as two containers each of rock, gravel and sand. When she poured the sand into the first cylinder, followed by the gravel, the rocks were too big to fit in the remaining space. Next she filled the second cylinder, first with the rocks, and then the gravel which filled the empty spaces, after which she poured in the sand. Her students were amazed that what would not fit into the first cylinder would fit into the second. Through this example they were able to understand the importance of order. In this case, the big things had to be put in first.

Life is no different. The big things must be considered first. If you just take things as they come, and never take time to sort them according to God's order, you will never get the important things to fit. Man is spirit, soul, and body, not body, soul, and spirit. His spirit must be considered first. If he has no respect for the creator, he will not have respect for the creation. Man's relationship with God is the foundation for his relationship with everyone else.

To determine if a man is ready for a committed relationship, the steps he has already taken must be evaluated. The making of a man is a part of the making of his relationship. They are interrelated. First God formed man out of dust and gave him a responsibility followed by accountability, both important steps in determining what sort of man he would become. The remainder of this chapter outlines five steps that a man must take to demonstrate that he is ready for you.

## STEP I: RESPONSIBILITY

*The LORD God took the man and put him in the Garden of Eden to work it and take care of it (Genesis 2:15).*

A woman should know if a man is responsible before she enters into a relationship with him. This is the first step to determining if he is "relationship ready." Work develops responsibility. Five of the most important words a woman can say to a man are "Do you have a job?" not because she wants to know how much he makes, but rather to determine whether or not he is experienced in shouldering responsibility.

It is best to find this out before emotions are involved because emotions can get in the way of good judgment.

Asking the question, "Do you have a job?" is a way of asking "Arc you responsible?" When a man does not work, there is no consistent measure of responsibility. If he is not responsible for himself, how will he be responsible for others? A man's ability to take care of himself is a vital part of who he is. He will never take the relationship seriously until he takes himself seriously. Man's relationship is tied to his sense of responsibility; therefore it is tied to his work. Both work and responsibility are measurable.

Work contributes to inner growth. Jesus referred to work as his spiritual food. "Jesus saith unto them, my meat is to do the will of him that sent me, and to finish his work" (John 4:34 KJV). The Apostle Paul referred to work as spiritual maturity. "For every one that useth milk is unskillful in the word of righteousness: for he is a babe but strong meat belongeth to them that are of full age" (Hebrews 5:13, 14 KJV).

Work allows us to see value in others. Men who work are more likely to value a woman than those who do not. "He that is faithful in that which is least is faithful also in much" (Luke 16:10 KJV). A man needs help when he is busy doing something productive. At the end of a hard day's work, he longs for someone to share in the fruit of his labor because God desires a man to be responsible. The very first thing God does for Adam after creating him was to give him the job of taking care of the Garden of Eden. Work is a very important part of the process. It is as natural to a man as eating. As a matter of fact, work is a prerequisite to eating. "For even when we were with you, we gave you this rule: "If a man will not work, he shall not eat" (II Thessalonians 3:10). Work is more than just a way of providing food for the table. It also supplies spiritual food.

## STEP II: ACCOUNTABILITY

*So then, each of us will give an account of himself to God. (Romans 14:12)*

Accountability is the second step in the process of demonstrating that a man is ready for you. No one is excluded from being accountable. Like responsibility, accountability precedes man's relationship. The way man pays his bills, gets to work on time, or attends worship service all give insight to how accountable he will be towards his relationship. The earth is the Lord's and everything in it. Man is a steward that must be accountable to the owner. "Know that the LORD is God. It is He who made us, and we are His; we are His people, the sheep of His pasture" (Psalms 100:3).

Accountability begins with keeping the commandment and obeying the laws of God, and man must acknowledge the existence of rules and/or boundaries or suffer the consequences. God told Adam that he could eat from every tree except for the one in the center of the garden, thus making him accountable. He would have to choose to obey and live forever in Eden or disobey and be expelled. Adam disobeyed and was expelled. Accountability carries very serious consequences. If a man refuses to be accountable, his life will be beset with difficulties. If you are in a relationship with him, your life will be hard as well.

Everyone is required to give an accounting for their actions, since responsibilities bring consequences. And the LORD God commanded the man, "You are free to eat from any tree in the garden; but you must not eat from the tree of the knowledge of good and evil, for when you eat of it you will surely die." (Genesis 2:16, 17). Life is full of "or else." Pay your utility bill or else your electricity will be turn off. Make your car payment or else your car will be repossessed. Man must be accountable or he will be force to live with the "or else," and so will those who are close to him.

Like responsibility, accountability precedes relationship. Accountability is one of the most important steps a man can take in demonstrating to God that he is ready for a healthy relationship. Adam blamed Eve, and Eve blamed the serpent, but this did not excuse their actions for they alone were responsible for their individual actions. No one is excluded from being accountable. Man is a steward of God, entrusted with the commandment, which is the word of God, and the garden that constitutes his immediate environment. The degree to which he is accountable in these respects will be a measure of his accountability in regard to everything.

## STEP III: SEE THE VALUE OF A MATE

*"Then the Lord God said, "It is not good for the man to be alone. I will make a helper who is just right for him." (Genesis 2:18 NLT)*

Man's attitude to marriage is a third measure of his responsibility, and it is another step in determining if he is ready for you. If he views marriage as a "ball and chain," he will also view his wife as a liability. A man who has failed to see the value of a mate has limited his own creativity and his own vision. “He who finds a wife finds what is good and receives favor from the LORD” (Proverbs 18:22).

God saw Adam’s needs through precept and example before Adam even realized that he had any. Although Adam was alone, he had no concept of being alone. Up to this point in Adam’s life, he had only experienced being with God. Adam’s time alone with God was a good thing, particularly since it allowed God to observe him. Because Adam was faithful in keeping the garden and the commandment, God deemed him relationship ready.

Man shows his future desire for a mate by his commitment to his present responsibilities. The Lord, impressed by Adam’s faithfulness, gave him more responsibility. “The LORD God said, “It is not good for the man to be alone. I will make a helper suitable for him.” (Genesis 2:18). When God saw Adam working alone, He decided that he needed a helpmate.

Man may not know what he needs, but God knows. Man demonstrates that he will value a mate by the value he places on himself. “Whoever can be trusted with very little can also be trusted with much, and whoever is dishonest with very little will also be dishonest with much” (Luke 16:10). If a man cannot be trusted with things that precede a committed relationship, he cannot be trusted with the relationship itself. Marriage requires preparation. Responsibility, accountability, and the acknowledgement of value in a mate are the first three steps to man demonstrating he is ready for a committed relationship.

## STEP IV: A DESIRE TO BE MARRIED

The fourth step in determining if he is ready involves a man's desire. It is not enough for a man to see the value of a mate. A man may see the value in a woman and still not desire to marry her. One would be mistaken in thinking that every man wants to be married. This is not automatic. Some men shy away from committed relationships. Relationships evolve from friendship, to dating, to engagement, to marriage. There is a time-period between a man seeing the value of a mate and actually desiring to commit to her.

A man who really wants a committed relationship will do the things necessary to prepare for it, including establishing himself in a job, acquiring suitable transportation, and becoming financially secure. The work a man does before the marriage will be the forerunner to the success of his marriage.

"And Adam gave names to all cattle, and to the fowl of the air, and to every beast of the field; but for Adam there was not found an help meet for him" (Genesis 2:20 KJV). God did not give Adam a mate after declaring it was not good for him to be alone because Adam was not ready for a mate at that time. He had more work to do. God instructed Adam to name the animals, all of whom existed in pairs. It was while doing this that Adam realized there was no one for him. The lion had a lioness, and the bear had a she-bear; only he was alone. It was at this point that Adam expresses his desire for a mate. He wanted someone like himself, and in recognizing this he took the first step to establishing a committed relationship.

You cannot be in a committed relationship with a man who does not desire to be in one with you. If his heart is not in it, he will, by default, mistreat you. His heart and his treasure will be elsewhere. "For where your treasure is, there your heart will be also" (Mathew 6:21 KJV).

Man's desire for a mate begins in his heart. If a man's heart is elsewhere, his treasure is elsewhere and mistreatment is inevitable. The desire for a mate will be demonstrated in a man's words and his actions. Jacob worked for his wife's hand in marriage for seven years and it seem like just a few days to him because he loved her so (Genesis 29:20).

## STEP V: GIVING PART OF YOURSELF

"Then the LORD God made a woman from the rib he had taken out of the man" (Genesis 2:22). The fifth and final way in which a man demonstrates that he is ready for a healthy relationship with you is the willingness to give a part of him. Adam proved himself responsible and accountable. He also saw the value of a mate. He went through the tedious process of naming all the animals before expressing his desire for his own mate. Adam would now make the ultimate sacrifice by giving a part of himself.

Just so, man cannot be in a committed relationship without giving up a part of himself. His emotions, heart and spirit must be shared. No one can become a part of him or his life without him sharing it. His time, energy, resources, talents, emotions, and desires must be given freely. Adam gave a rib from his side. Eve had his heart before she had his rib. No man will make that level of sacrifice without his heart being committed. Because of this, Adam would forever be connected with Eve. His commitment to her could not be questioned.

Great relationships evolve from great commitment. Taking

on responsibility, accepting accountability, seeing value in a mate, desiring a mate, and giving of oneself are all key elements that demonstrate a man is ready for this commitment. Men must take all these steps in order for any relationship to be stable. Removing any one step is like removing one of the pillars that support the bridge; the whole structure becomes unstable. The willingness of a man to share is heart is the final step.

## WILLINGNESS TO GIVE

To have a healthy relationship, men today must be willing to give a part of themselves. They must be willing to give their hands, heart, back, and brain, forsaking all others for the good of the relationship. These men must be willing to join heart and soul with their wives. "For this reason a man will leave his father and mother and be united to his wife, and they will become one flesh" (Genesis 2:24).

A man's willingness to give everything but his heart speaks volume about how he views the relationship. Man is a spirit, therefore; he is spiritual. A man's heart is where spiritual oneness takes place. This is the most important part of who he is. A man gives his heart and spirit in expression of the final step to commitment. The value a man sees in himself is the value he will see in the relationship.

The oneness between man and woman is sanctioned by God. It is spiritual. If man is not ready for it, God will not give it to him. This limits that relationship to the physical and emotional realm, both temporal environments. Physical appearances and emotions change but the spirit of man is eternal. Real relationships require a spiritual connection.

Adam called Eve "bone of his bone and flesh of his flesh." (Genesis 2:23). She was just as much a part of him as he was of himself. This is the basis of a healthy relationship. When a man gives a part of himself, he forms a lasting bond. His time, energy, resources, passions, affections, and commitment are connected to the relationship. He sees his woman as a part of him. She is bone of his bone and flesh of his flesh and there is no one closer.

Man will always be more that what meets the eye. He is a body and soul whose spirit best represents his true self. His spirit is the essence of who he is, and it will ultimately determine how he will behave. The physical and mental characteristics of a man will always be secondary to his spirit which generates how he thinks and acts. Understanding man's connection to dirt, gives you spiritual insight that will change you, your relationships, and your life!

# About the Author

TIMOTHY Houston is the owner of Houston Publishing, a family-owned publishing company that is committed to producing life-changing Christian books. His first book, *Study to Be Quiet* provides the reader with important insights regarding the ways of creating the right environment to hear from God during the times of crisis. Tim also is a motivational speaker, and has participated in ministries throughout the USA, and also in Japan and Korea. He brings a wealth of knowledge gained though twenty-five years of Christian ministry, as well as thirteen years of leadership in the United States Marines. Raised in Saginaw, Michigan, Tim now lives in Minneapolis, Minnesota where he currently worships at Greater Saint Paul Church of God in Christ.

Get a copy of Tim Houston other book
"Study to Be Quiet"
Visit our website at: www.menaredirt.com

For booking and speaking engagements contact us at:
www.menaredirt.com

To order a books, tapes, or to obtain additional information about the author, visit our website at:
www.menaredirt.com